AF526422

THE CRIMSON WEB OF TERROR

by Robert D. Chapman
and M. Lester Chapman

The Crimson Web of Terror
by Robert D. Chapman and M. Lester Chapman

ISBN 0-87364-187-6
Printed in the United States of America

Published by Paladin Press, a division of
Paladin Enterprises, Inc., P.O. Box 1307,
Boulder, Colorado 80306, USA.
(303) 443-7250

Direct inquiries and/or orders to the above address.

Dedicated to Leslie Philandra

When we agree that the cause is noble, we are tempted to condone the terror. But are we wise to do so? The act we condone today may be the one we regret tomorrow, for terrorism in the end affects everyone; it is an attack on civilization at large. Violence breeds violence, murder answers murder and order dissolves in chaos.

Mitchell Sharp
Canada's Secretary of States
for External Affairs
Address to General Assembly,
United Nations, 1972

Contents

Introduction

Many criminologists and other experts believe terrorism to be a phenomenon. *The Crimson Web Of Terror* will show that it is not. Others regard terrorists as psychological misfits; they are not and this will also be shown. Some believe terrorism arises from social and economic issues and that if these problems are solved, terrorism will go away. It will not, because terrorism is a form of insurgency.

Terrorist-insurgency is the most effective war waged since the days of Alexander the Great. Africa, South of the Sahara, including the strategic Horn of Africa, is lost to the West. Southeast Asia is in enemy hands. Afghanistan and Iran are all but lost. The Mideast from Turkey to the Persian Gulf is in a precarious situation, and probably cannot hold out over the long run. The Caribbean is slipping away. Central America probably will be lost by the summer of 1981. All are victims of the undeclared war of terrorism. *The Crimson Web Of Terror* describes how these small groups of terrorist-revolutionaries, a mere handful of men, are conquering the world.

In Mr. Chapman's 27 years with the Central Intelligence Agency his assignments were mostly in countries with terrorist and insurgency problems. He knew terrorists intimately. He interrogated them. He operated against them as they did against him. He was a prisoner of revolutionaries. He also negotiated the release of American hostages. From these experiences, he acquired knowledge, both operational and security-oriented, of how to cope with and defend against terrorist attacks.

In 1970 when Daniel Mitrione was murdered in Montevideo by the Tupamaros, Chapman was assigned to formulate defense tactics against terrorist attacks. The program was highly successful as he helped put together training courses for officers assigned to high risk areas.

He later briefed foreign police and security services in over twenty foreign countries in these tactics. He lectured on terrorism to CIA officers as well as selected federal officials going on overseas assignments. Today Mr. Chapman still lectures on the subject to U.S. military officers.

Long before Mr. Chapman retired from the agency, he was aware that while he could teach defensive tactics against terrorists to foreign police and security services, U.S. legal peculiarities prohibited a CIA officer from passing along the same information to police forces in the U.S. or to the American business community.

In *The Crimson Web Of Terror* we have tried to fill this void. The book includes a great deal of the information that Mr. Chapman gave to foreign policemen and security officials who deal with terrorist activities on a daily basis. Supplemental information is included from his present activities. He is employed as a risk analyst, compiling a worldwide data base on the world's terrorist and insurgent groups. He also works as a free lance security consultant and in this capacity investigates insurance companies' insured risks in areas of insurgency. By these means, he has been able to stay current on terrorists and the tactics they use.

The Publishers
May, 1980

1

The Act of Terror

A hijacked Lufthansa plane, flight 181, sat on the Aden runway October 16, 1978. Inside the terrorist leader, Juhair Akkash, using the alias "Captain Walter Mahmud," was angered by the German pilot, Juergen Schumann. Schumann was provoking Akkash by refusing to cooperate. The terrorist arrogantly summoned Schumann to him, and forced him to kneel. Akkash then fired a fatal bullet between Schumann's eyes. The passengers were terrorized.

To understand actions such as Akkash's, terrorism itself must first be understood.

The Terrorist Act

The terrorist act begins when a violent yet vague plan forms in the terrorist's mind involving a predetermined victim. The victim is surveilled, the terrorist gathers intelligence on the victim, and an ambush site is selected. Terrorists then visit the ambush location and decide how to commit the crime. They will practice the act on the spot so they will be able to commit it with precision in the shortest time possible. Once the act is carried out, it is no longer a secret. Government reacts and the police and security forces respond. If it is a hostage situation, a command center is established and negotiations begin. After the incident is over, police and security officers draft post-incident reports and list their successes and failures. The knowledge gained will be used the next time a terrorist attacks.

There is certain to be a next time because terror has proved to be an effective weapon. Eighty percent of all terrorists' acts are successful.

One reason for their success is because of the secrecy and stealth observed in the preparation and execution of a terrorist act. Carlos

Marighella, the Brazilian terrorist, wrote in his *Mini-Manual of the Urban Guerrilla:* "We (the terrorists) determine the hour and place of attack, fix its duration and establish its objective. The enemy remains ignorant."

As with the hunter and the hunted, the advantage is with the hunter. If he is determined, it is difficult to stop him. If kidnapping is impossible, the terrorist resorts to assassination. If his selected victim is protected, the terrorist shifts his attack to the victim's wife and children. If ransom is paid, the terrorist wins his point. If ransom is not paid, the terrorist kills the hostage and walks away triumphantly because he has propagandized his capability to terrorize, to intimidate and to subjugate.

Origins of U.S. Policy

In 1970, the U.S. government first became deeply concerned and involved in international terrorism and its threat to U.S. officials serving abroad.

In that year a U.S. public safety official, Daniel Mitrione, who was assigned to the embassy in Montevideo, Uruguay, was kidnapped by the Tupamaros, a Uruguayan terrorist group. When kidnapped, Mitrione was hit on the head, thrown into a truck and without reason, shot in the side. Later he was imprisoned in an underground pit where he was tied to a cot and blindfolded. He remained in the pit for several weeks. Finally, he was interrogated and taken outside the city where he was shot in the head two times with a .45 caliber pistol. On hearing of this atrocity, most U.S. officials serving in Latin America bought a gun and said they would sooner take a bullet by fighting or running away than die as Mitrione died.

The following excerpts are from a tape of Mitrione's interrogation by the Tupamaros:

Mitrione: "I spend 99 percent of my time in the embassy."

Tupamaro: "Yes I think my mates know that, because they have been checking everything about you for a long time."

(This revealed that the Tupamaros undertook casings and surveillance of the victim before the kidnapping.)

Tupamaro: "There in the police station you have a place to park your car, down there in the garage. I know."

(Undoubtedly they surveilled even the police garage.)

Tupamaro: "Yes I do know but you know we changed places. Now I am the police."

Tupamaro: "Yes we read all those documents you sent to the local police departments in Latin America."

Mitrione: "Well they are changing that now."

Tupamaro: "We have been reading the manual on interrogation. That is very interesting."

(Mitrione was debriefed by the terrorists who used the police manuals he had supplied to the police department.)

At that point the tape ended.

Mitrione's murder was so brutal that it shocked the U.S. Government into action. I was given the problem at that time of creating a defense doctrine for the protection of U.S. officers in Latin America against terrorism. From this beginning, a counterterrorist tactics course was organized for U.S. officers going overseas.

Preventative Measures

The point is that a potential victim cannot sit by and do nothing, because by doing nothing he signals to the terrorist that he is an easy mark. There are preventative measures that can and should be taken.

1. The victim can take personal security measures to make the terrorist's act difficult for him to commit.
2. He can practice physical security in his home and in his office, making a special effort to change his home from a trap to a fortress. For instance, lights shining on entrances and exits are effective deterrents to terrorists and burglars as well.
3. The use of a weapon by a victim adds risk to the terrorist, and if the terrorist persists in trying to kill, he may lose his own life.

The most elementary part of personal security is prior planning. Prior planning is to know in advance what to do if something happens.

An example of prior planning is to own a dog. Not that the dog will attack the intruder, but its bark will give a warning. A barking dog will give 60 to 120 seconds reaction time. When the dog barks, the intended victim should get out of bed, get his gun, cock it, put a chair against the door and telephone the police, keeping the gun aimed at the door. The dog's one or two minute warning can make the difference in saving a lifc.

Prior planning also calls for a working knowledge of defensive driving techniques. However, defensive driving does not begin at the scene of the ambush and blockade. It begins when the driver enters his car.

Defensive drivers should vary their routine of travel from home to office and office to home, because when the terrorist observes routine he can select an ambush site for the purpose of abduction or murder. If the route is changed constantly, the terrorist is hard pressed to find a suitable ambush site. He has to return to the victim's neighborhood to attack him. But by prior planning, the intended victim knows the area near his home *better* than the terrorist does. This can be an important advantage.

Defensive drivers must be observant at all times. When something out of the ordinary appears, be it a checkpoint, accident, or abandoned car, the defensive driver should back up and take another route.

Learning from Experience

Counterterrorists have learned from past acts of terrorism. For example, Brazilian diplomats were ambushed, shot and kidnapped while in cars. The following experiences added valuable lessons to counterterrorists' knowledge.

In the kidnapping of U.S. Ambassador Burke Elbrick in Rio de Janeiro, investigation showed that witnesses saw the terrorists loitering in the ambush area for several days before the kidnapping took place. One witness called the police and reported the terrorists as suspicious characters but no investigation was carried out. The terrorists were casing the area and "dry-running" their action.

There was a positive note in the attempted kidnapping of American Consul Curtis Cutter in Port Alegre. Cutter escaped. During the post-incident investigation, he attributed his escape to the fact that he had definitely decided to try to escape if a kidnapping attempt was made against him. So when Cutter saw the ambush in front of him, he did not have to make up his mind. He accelerated and rammed the blocking vehicles, running over one terrorist and breaking his leg.

One of the kidnapper's shots went through Cutter's rear window and wounded him in the shoulder. The wound was preferable to falling into the hands of the terrorists.

The kidnapping of Japanese Counsel Nobuo Okushi in Sao Paulo, Brazil, took less than a minute. It was carried out with precision by at least seven men. An ice cream vendor remembered having seen these same men in the area on the previous two days.

During the kidnapping of Swiss Ambassador Giovanni Enrico Bucher in Rio de Janeiro, the Ambassador's guard, riding in the front seat, tried to draw his pistol but wasn't able to do so. The guard was shot three times in the back by a third man who approached the car from the right rear and fired through an open window. Again the operation took only slightly more than one minute to execute. The Ambassador had been asked to increase his guards, as he was known to be a possible terrorist target, but refused. Instead Bucher often went driving in a small sports car accompanied by only one guard.

Similar tactics are used in all kidnap and assassination cases where the victim's car is ambushed. The same tactics used against Elbrick, Nobuo and Bucher were used later by the Red Brigades of Italy and the Baader-Meinhoff gang of West Germany.

Terrorists are not fools. They are intelligent people, devising tactics by which they can more easily attack their victims. By using intelligence, even hard targets, such as armed policemen, are attacked with minimum danger to the terrorists.

In the United States, terrorists have telephoned for police assistance. Responding officers were ambushed and killed. Another terrorist tactic is to commit a minor driving violation, and when stopped by police, kill the unsuspecting officers.

Terrorists in the United States have successfully used the panel truck as an attack vehicle. They pile sandbags along the inside of the truck, converting it into a homemade armored car. Also in the United States, terrorists have geared assassinations to the cold weather cycle so that overcoats and loose outer clothing can be used to conceal automatic weapons and shotguns. The victim can then be murdered at point-blank range.

In Turkey, there was an attempted kidnapping of a U.S. AID official. He was living on the fourth floor of an apartment building. At nine o'clock one night, he opened the door in response to a knock.

Four terrorists charged into the room waving pistols. They pistol-whipped him. As he screamed for help, his thirteen-year-old son came to his rescue. The boy grabbed an ornamental sword and swung it through the air. He hit one or two of the terrorists and they fled. The thwarted terrorists had intended to knock the official out, roll him in a rug, and carry him out of the building.

Investigators found that the night chain on the official's apartment door had not been fastened. Had the AID official used it, he might possibly have spared himself a very bad experience. The point is that the use of security equipment is imperative.

Most people believe that a terrorist act will never affect them. This is perhaps a logical conclusion based upon the law of averages, but once a terrorist situation develops, it is too late to make plans. The initial reaction is shock. There are only seconds to make a decision. Prior planning is therefore vital.

The options are to surrender or to escape either by defensive driving techniques, or by shooting it out with the assailants. But let us assume the assailants are professionals and the intended victim is completely boxed-in. There is no chance to use defensive driving techniques. The victim is kidnapped.

U.S. Negotiation Policy

The host government will begin to make post-incident responses. The first consideration is what your government will do to help. You are an American citizen; what can you expect?

Upon being informed that you have been kidnapped by terrorists, the United States government will stand back and authorize the host government to conduct negotiations on your behalf.

The rationale for this U.S. policy relies on the Vienna Convention of 1924. This convention states that the host country is responsible for all people living within its boundaries. In other words, it is the responsibility of the host country to get you out of trouble.

The policy was reemphasized by former Secretary of State Henry Kissinger. Since that time United States policy has precluded direct negotiations with terrorists who hold U.S. officials. It also rules out the payment of ransom. In August 1975 the United States Ambassador in Tanzania was recalled and demoted. He was demoted because he negotiated the private payment of ransom for the release of three U.S. students who were taken hostage in Zaire.

There are pros and cons to this policy, which was again confirmed in President Carter's Presidential Review Memorandum #30.

The policy is not a bad one. It provides a buffer between the U.S. government and the terrorists, and it is advantageous to deal through a buffer. If the U.S. adopted a policy of direct negotiation and paying ransoms, there would be even more kidnappings of U.S. officials, with progressively higher ransom demands. The lives of U.S. officials would be in greater jeopardy, not less.

I have learned from my experiences that American diplomats are generally not good negotiators. They are just not experienced enough or tough enough.

A hostage should hope that the negotiator is some wily European or Mideastern diplomat or government official who has haggled for survival all his life.

When a U.S. official is kidnapped, the U.S. government does the following:

1. It offers the host country assistance and advice, intelligence, equipment, and technical services. It will help find contacts on behalf of the host government. The host government can accept or reject this aid.
2. The U.S. will not counsel the host government on how to respond. (In practice it does.)
3. If ransom is demanded, the U.S. will remind the host government that it does not pay ransom.
4. If the host government wishes to pay the ransom, the U.S. Government will take a neutral position.
5. If a private U.S. company wishes to pay the ransom, the U.S. Government will advise that the demand should not be met but will take a neutral stand.
6. If the host government does not wish to act, the U.S. Government will nominate an intermediary to the host government.
7. If all recourse to the above is negative, the U.S. Government will then step in.

A problem was raised in the Leonhardy kidnap case in Guadalajara. The terrorists were in contact with the victim's wife by telephone and passed messages to her. It was decided that this did not violate the rule prohibiting negotiating with terrorists. Henceforth, American officials could become involved in the negotiating process if they are "conveyors of information," but not negotiators.

The Military Option

There is also the "military option," meaning the use of a military force to release hostages as the Israelis did in Entebbe and the West Germans in Mogadiscio.

After the success of Entebbe, the United States responded to public concern and organized a strike force code named *Delta.* Organized after the British SAS and the German GSG-9, Delta's striking feature is that it is a self-contained unit with its own supporting logistical system. It is a "low visibility" force. By military definition, a "low visibility" force differs from a clandestine or covert force in that once deployed the United States Government cannot deny responsibility.

Low visibility includes operations such as Mogadiscio, where the German team arrived in Somalia with the consent of the Somalian government. It does not involve "high visibility" Entebbe-type operations in which the host government is hostile to the rescue team. The underlying problem with military option teams is the risk involved in rescue.

When the Israeli government gave the green light to the Entebbe operation, they were willing to accept troop and hostage casualties of over fifty percent. The political feasibility of such a high-risk rescue operation is doubtful in the United States. Now, after Mogadiscio, the risks are even greater. The terrorists are aware of the military option. They rig explosives in the hijacked plane and drench the interior with gasoline. The risk has grown to such an extent that the military option may no longer be an option.

However, if a military option is used, it must be used without constraints. With any delay, the risk that the terrorists will kill the hostages increases so rapidly that it undermines the whole purpose of rescue. This is the greatest danger in the formation of a military option force.

In hostage situations, rescue planners construct a mockup of the plane or building where the hostages are held. If it is a plane, they will study the engineering specifications of that particular type of aircraft. If it is a building, such as the airport terminal at Entebbe, the planners will interview everybody they can locate who has ever been in the building. Every detail is important.

During the Entebbe incident, the terrorists released the non-Jewish hostages and they were flown to Paris. In Paris they were met by a group of Israeli intelligence officers and debriefed. The following was the basic debriefing guide used by the Israeli intelligence officers:

1. The exact location of the hostages.
2. Number of terrorists.
3. Routine of hostages and terrorists.
4. Degree of cooperation between the host country and the terrorists.
5. Internal to external arrangements (diagram) of where the hostages were held, identifying all points of entry and exit.
6. Location of electric circuits and fuse boxes.

As the freed hostages were debriefed, the intelligence was relayed to the planners in Tel Aviv, where the information was factored into the mockup, and strategy and tactics were revised.

Several lessons were learned from the Entebbe experience. One was that in hostage situations there is a tremendous need for intelligence.

Second, if at all possible, secure the release of one or more hostages for intelligence purposes, or, alternatively, put someone inside.

Third, hostages should observe everything around them. If released, they can then give the information to the rescuers.

When a kidnapping takes place, the victim usually suffers more from shock and fear than any real physical injury. He should think escape, and first assess his physical condition. Then he should check what he has on his person that might be useful. A two inch hacksaw blade, concealed either in a shoe or wallet, is a versatile tool that will cut through rope, a lock, or a metal bar.

The best opportunity to escape usually comes during the first few moments of captivity. At that time the captors are occupied with their own escape from the scene. Brief opportunities to escape may occur during these first few hectic minutes. The chances for escape become fewer and farther apart the longer the victim is in enemy hands.

Hostage Conduct

Abduction and imprisonment are a debilitating experience for the hostage. How should he conduct himself while imprisoned? The victim can conquer debilitation by remaining mentally alert. Listen and remember as much detailed information as possible. Exercise to maintain your strength.

Interrogation is an aspect of kidnapping that is particularly harrowing. The terrorists are not experienced interrogators and are unaware of subtle interrogation methods. The terrorists will threaten torture. The most common form of torture used by terrorists is beating.

It is necessary, however, to differentiate between torture and the threat of torture. In most kidnap cases, the threat is almost always made but not always carried out. The threat of torture is a standard operational procedure used by terrorists as a psychological tool against the captive. In such cases the individual decides when he is at the breaking point. Outward signs of fear or even an apparent lack of resolve will encourage terrorists to make good their threats.

Several years ago in Peru two police officers were captured by guerrillas. Reasonably treated at first, they were required to teach basic marksmanship to their captors. The policemen became friendly with the guerrillas. After a few weeks passed the guerrillas began to abuse and taunt them. The policemen begged for mercy. From that point on, the situation deteriorated rapidly. They were tortured, with each guerrilla trying to outdo the other in inflicting intense pain. The prisoners suffered a lingering death.

Subsequently one of the guerrillas who was an active participant in the torture of the policemen was captured. His interrogation showed that the guerrillas had not intended to abuse the prisoners at first, but that the obvious fear shown by them encouraged the torture sessions that followed.

Courage will not prevent torture, but its absence may encourage terrorists to begin abuses which lead to torture. There are several lessons to be learned from this particular incident:

1. Do not offer cooperation beyond that which may be absolutely necessary to exist.

2. Remain composed and aloof.

3, Do not enter into discussion or polemics. There is no chance of converting the captors. Any attempt to become friendly with the captors will bring contempt.

The question is asked whether the last sentence contradicts the *Stockholm Syndrome.* It does not because the Stockholm Syndrome applies only to hostage-barricade situations where the police have encircled the place where the terrorists are holding the hostages. In such cases both the terrorists and the hostages have a common fear that the police will break in shooting and kill both terrorists and hostages. The terrorists and the hostages now find that they have something in common and that the police outside are a common enemy. In the Peruvian case, as in most terrorist kidnappings, the hostages were held in the terrorist camp without a surrounding police force. These are not hostage-barricade situations.

2

Policy, Diplomacy and Terrorism

I have been a counterterrorist for twenty years. For most of this time, the political considerations which influenced my job were few. If a terrorist threw a bomb, killed a policeman, or hijacked a plan, he was an enemy. The United States government lent its resources to help friendly governments prevent political overthrow by terrorist groups. Political considerations elevated counterterrorism from a police mission to a mission of state.

Prior to 1976 whenever a friendly government was attacked by terrorists, the United States government made available money, equipment, and counterterrorist experts to help put down the insurgency. But most importantly, the United States publicly gave its moral backing to the government under attack. The besieged government knew it was not alone. The U.S. agencies worked with the local security services to combat the terrorist threat. They had three fundamental counterterrorist missions. The first was to penetrate the terrorist's organization and collect information on its leaders and members, the organization of its support apparatus, and the identification of those who belonged to it; and learn the identity of any terrorist targets so that they could be protected. The second mission was to see to it that the acquired information was passed on to the appropriate local police authorities so they could arrest and detain the terrorists. The third mission was to pass the details of the police arrests and detentions to newspapers in order to publicize the terrorists' failures, deterring others from joining the terrorists' organizations.

Yet since the Vietnam war, and the press and congressional uproar over the CIA's covert involvement in bringing about the downfall of the Chilean communist regime of Salvador Allende, the United States government has changed its policy. It will no longer help friendly governments to counter terrorist attacks. America will not give another country any type of offensive help to combat terrorist attacks, even though the terrorists were trained and supplied by the Soviet Union or Cuba. Simply stated, the United States government does not want to become involved in a situation comparable to its previous involvement in Chile. It will take no action to suppress a local political group even though that political group is also a terrorist organization.

The New U.S. Policy

The previous policy of helping friendly governments under terrorist attack has been replaced by a new policy premised on the assumption that the U.S. can no longer achieve its political and economic goals abroad by military power or by economic pressure. Instead of military force or economic coercion, the United States government is now trying to adapt with and guide the world's revolutionary movements so that they are more compatible with America's national interests. This was summed up by Secretary of State Cyrus Vance, "The United States must accept the fact that other societies will manage change and build new institutions in patterns that may be different from our own. Our national interest is not in all countries becoming like us. It is that they be free of domination by others."

The most recent and perhaps best example of this policy occurred in Nicaragua. There the United States government helped the Sandinist National Liberation Front (FSLN) topple the government of Anastasio Somoza. In an interview on September 6, 1979 three time former Costa Rican President Jose Figueres explained the Havana-San Jose air route which for months supplied the FSLN with weapons and supplies. He said, "We reached such insolence that a Cuban air route supplying arms to the guerrilla army operated in Costa Rica." He then disclosed, "When the Sandinists still had a long way to go between La Virgen, near the Costa Rican border, and Managua, U.S. President Jimmy Carter reached an agreement with

Fidel Castro to prolong the affair and permit the military strengthening of the Sandinists."

It is only natural that with this dramatic change in policy, and while the United States contacts insurgent leaders, the word "counterterrorism" is frowned upon in Washington. And as a result most counterterrorists in government service have resigned or retired. Insurgency not only increased throughout the world, but terrorists also assumed a moralistic political position. Terrorists began to claim that theirs was an inherent right to wage revolution and that terror was a weapon of revolution. Anyone who sought to restrict, constrain, counter or destroy this use of terror violated the rights of revolutionaries to be free. They found support for this moralistic position in the Declaration of the United Nations, Resolution 1514, "The Terrorist Manifesto." It reads:

"All people have the right to self-determination—for the subjection of people to alien subjugation, domination and exploitation constitutes a denial of human rights and is contrary to the charter of the United Nations and is an impediment to the promotion of world peace and cooperation."

To many people, perhaps half of the world's population, this declaration means that police action to nullify terrorism as a revolutionary tactic to end "alien subjection, domination and exploitation" is a denial of human rights. Because of this widespread belief, about one-third to one-half of the members of the United Nations condone the use of terror. It is also impossible for the Western world to obtain any kind of a ruling which would classify the act of terrorism as an international crime. To obtain such a ruling would require many countries, Cuba and Libya to mention only two, to change their foreign policies which are based upon revolution and terrorism.

This could be the end of the matter. The United States could absolutely refuse to be involved in any political situation associated with terrorism, insurgency, or revolution. It could bury its head in the sand and refuse to take cognizance of what is happening. But unfortunately, these same revolutionary and insurgent groups reach out and commit terrorist acts against Americans. When this happens, the United States government adjusts its policy and views such acts against its citizens as acts of "international terrorism." In such instances the United States will provide defensive (but not offensive) aid to the country where acts of international terrorism occur.

International Terrorism

For an act of terrorism to be considered an act of international terrorism, thereby classifying its perpetrator as an international terrorist organization, the act of terror must contain three essential elements: 1) It must be an act of violence; 2) It must have been committed for political, economic or social reasons; and 3) It must transcend international boundaries. All three of these elements must be present in an act of international terror. If one element is missing, the act is one of local or internal terrorism rather than international terrorism, and no support or assistance can be expected from the United States. The definition is difficult and presents a number of problems in determining whether a terrorist act is indeed international.

The following examples may be of assistance in making a determination: 1) When terrorists explode a bomb in a building or a place which they know that Americans frequent, it is an act of international terrorism. The act transcends international boundaries. 2) When terrorists kidnap an American businessman in a foreign country and hold him for ransom in order to carry on their revolutionary activities, this, too, transcends international boundaries and is an act of international terrorism. 3) The hijacking of an international airliner is an act of international terrorism. However, when a revolutionary group obtains weapons supplied by a foreign power and uses the weapons to kill a local politician, this does not transcend international boundaries and is an act of local terrorism.

To date, thirty-two revolutionary groups have struck out at foreigners and are now labeled as international terrorists. These groups are:

1. Baader-Meinhoff/Red Army Faction — Germany.
2. 2 June Movement — Germany.
3. Revolutionary Cells — Germany.
4. Croatian Separatists — Europe.
5. Armenian Liberation Army — Europe.
6. South Moluccans — Netherlands.
7. Red Resistance Front — Netherlands.

8. 17 November Group — Greece.
9. Turkish People's Liberation Party/Front (TPLP/F) Swift Ones — Turkey.
10. Movement for the Self-Determination and Independence of the Canary Archipelago (MPAIAC) — Canary Islands

The determination which found the MPAIAC to be an international terrorist organization came in 1978. The MPAIAC had planted a small bomb in a flower shop in the concourse of the Las Palmas airport in the Canary Islands. After the ensuing explosion, Spanish authorities feared additional bombings and rerouted all international flights from Las Palmas to the nearby Tenerife airport. The following morning two planes collided on the Tenerife runway, resulting in history's worst airline disaster.

The United States government found a chain of causation between the flower shop bomb and the airline collision. They determined the MPAIAC to be an international terrorist organization.

The list continues:

11. Popular Front for the Liberation of Palestine (PFLP) — Mideast.
12. Black September Organization (BSO) — Mideast.
13. Popular Front for the Liberation of Palestine — General Command (PFLP — GC) — Mideast.
14. Black June — Mideast.
15. Front of the Liberation of Palestine (FLP) — Mideast.
16. Arab Liberation Front (FLP) — Mideast.
17. Japanese Red Army (JRA) — Mideast.
18. New People's Army — Philippines.
19. Moro National Liberation Front (MNLF) — Philippines.
20. Guerrilla Army of the Poor (EGP) — Guatemala.
21. Revolutionary Armed Forces (FAR) — Guatemala.
22. People's Liberation Army (EPL) — Colombia.
23. Colombia Revolutionary Armed Forces (FARC) — Colombia.
24. Sandinist National Liberation Front (FSLN) — Nicaragua.

25. Revolutionary Coordinating Junta (JCR) — Southern Cone of Latin America.
26. People's Revolutionary Army (ERP) — Argentina.
27. Montoneros — Argentina.
28. Tupamaros — Uruguay.
29. 23 September Communist League (23 SCL) — Mexico.
30. Union of the People (UDP) — Mexico.
31. People's Strugglers — Iran.
32. People's Sacrifice Guerrillas — Iran.

It would appear that since these thirty-two organizations are classified as international terrorists, the United States government would assist other countries in trying to control them. The United States government does not do so because of an intervening human rights policy. If the terrorists operate from inside a country which has a human rights issue—the People's Strugglers in Iran provide an excellent example—the United States will not help that country because of the possibility that those terrorists who are apprehended will be mistreated. This policy affects sixteen of the thirty-two international terrorist organizations. They are:

1. Turkish People's Liberation Party Front.
2. New People's Army.
3. Moro National Liberation Front.
4. Guerrilla Army of the Poor.
5. Revolutionary Armed Forces.
6. People's Liberation Army.
7. Colombia Revolutionary Armed Forces.
8. Sandinist National Liberation Front.
9. Revolutionary Coordinating Junta.
10. People's Revolutionary Army.
11. Montomeros.
12. Tupamaros.
13. 23 September Communist League.
14. Union of the People.
15. People's Strugglers.
16. People's Sacrifice Guerrillas.

This leaves sixteen groups against whom action might be taken. But of these sixteen, seven are headquartered and operate from sanctuaries where the local government supports terrorism. It is impossible to undertake any action against these seven international terrorist organizations which are:

1. Popular Front for the Liberation of Palestine.
2. Black September Organization.
3. Popular Front for the Liberation of Palestine — General Command.
4. Black June.
5. Front for the Liberation of Palestine.
6. Arab Liberation Front.
7. Japanese Red Army.

Thus, in the final analysis, there are nine organizations of international terrorists against whom the United States could take some type of action. These are:

1. Baader-Meinhoff Gang — Red Army Faction.
2. 2 June Movement.
3. Revolutionary Cells.
4. Armenian Liberation Army.
5. South Moluccans.
6. Red Resistance Front.
7. 17 November Group.
8. Croatian Separatists.
9. Movement for the Self-Determination and Independence of the Canary Archipelago.

There is yet one more limitation. The United States will not deliver a terrorist into the hands of another country unless that country has a legal cause of action against the terrorist. For example, only Germany can claim custody of Abu Daud for the Olympic massacre. There are few other terrorists, perhaps four to six against whom such legal action is pending.

In Washington the management of the war against terrorism has become a bureaucracy within a bureaucracy. The Working Group on Terrorism of the Special Coordinating Committee of the National Security Council (NSC/SCC/WIG), is charged with the war against terrorism. It is made up of representatives from twenty-nine different agencies and departments and is too unwieldly to do more than discuss matters of general interest. The NSC/SCC/WIG has had to delegate downward.

The next step down is the Executive Committee, which is headed by a Department of State officer of ambassadorial rank. Under the Executive Committee is a growing proliferation of subordinate committees and subcommittees which now number seventeen in all. Little is accomplished, yet the officer in charge can do little with twenty-nine different agencies, to manage, each pulling for their own parochial and often conflicting interests. The chairmanship of the Executive Committee has changed five times during the past two years.

In recent years policy and diplomacy toward terrorism has become complicated. As a result, the mission of a counterterrorist has become more limited and ineffective.

3
Terrorist Theory

To preface this important chapter, allow me to briefly outline some of my personal counterterrorist experiences.

Throughout the Cuban revolution, I was in Santiago de Cuba and Havana. I arrived in Santo Domingo the day after Trujillo was assassinated. I went there for a week but stayed through six months of chaos, and then returned during the Dominican Revolution of 1965. I followed Cuba's export of the revolution to Latin America, and was assigned to Brazil in time to observe the rise of Carlos Marighella and his Cuban style of urban terrorism. During a recent assignment I worked with the Israelis and became enmeshed in Palestine terrorism. I have had a long, close confrontation with terrorism and terrorist. I have known terrorists and I have operated against them.

The Cuban Revolution

During this close contact I have witnessed the development of terrorism into a form of revolution. Twenty years ago terror was only a tactic of revolution. But from the tactical use of terror in the Cuban revolution it has become, step by step, the revolution itself. It is too commonly said that terrorism is a phenomenon. I do not find this so because terrorism has been present for centuries. However, before Castro, terrorism was a random act. When Fidel Castro and his handful of men invaded Oriente Province, Cuba, in 1956 they were nearly annihilated in a firefight with the Cuban Army. The survivors fled to the Sierra Maestra Mountains where Castro sat on the mountain top. He was a revolutionary, surrounded by the Cuban Army, and on the plains below there was not a sign of revolution. The popular uprisings which were to have coincided with Castro's invasion had not materialized.

An ordinary revolutionary would have retreated to a place of safety to try again some other time, but Castro was not an ordinary revolutionary. He was a tenacious man. Secondly, he could not retreat—he was on an island surrounded by an army. There was no place to go. He had two choices. He could surrender or he could try to survive. He chose survival. Yet Castro felt that he had to carry his fight, somehow, into the cities and the countryside. He could not win a revolution sitting on a mountain top. Castro's revolutionaries began to implement two innovative tactics from their stronghold, one in the rural areas and the other in the cities.

On the rural front the revolutionaries were weak in manpower and firepower. Any attack against the enemy required the concentration of their entire force on one single objective at a time. They assembled into small groups, called "columns." Using the tactics of stealth they ambushed or attacked small, outnumbered military guardposts. Immediately following the attack, before a larger military force could pursue them, the column retreated back into their mountain sanctuary. Only on rare occasions, when the column was intercepted in its retreat march, was the Cuban army able to inflict casualties upon the rebel forces. In this way the Cuban revolution was fought. It was like a gnat darting out and biting a giant, until finally the morale of the giant collapsed.

The warfare in the cities was waged by the revolutionary underground, the 26th of July Movement. The underground was small in number, middle class in origin, and dedicated to their cause. They were of the same composition as today's urban terrorist.

The mission of the urban underground was to make the world aware that there was a revolution in Cuba. In essence, the 26th of July Movement had to make a revolution where none existed. They had to produce overt manifestations of an abnormal, revolutionary situation. To do this, the underground used terror as its tool. Under penalty of death, the 26th of July Movement prohibited Cubans from attending movies, parties, or any amusement or social diversion. The country and its people could not appear happy; they had to appear as if they were in the middle of a revolution. Bright clothing was frowned upon, black clothing was preferred by Castro. The populace was terrorized into not going out at night. Those who put up

Christmas decorations were ordered to dismantle them on threat of being bombed.

Society became disrupted and the appearance of revolution grew. Kidnappings took place with publicity as the ransom, not money. Juan Fangio, the Argentine race driver, was kidnapped in Havana. Nine American engineers were taken on the North Coast. Twenty-nine American sailors and marines were kidnapped on the South Coast, outside the Guantanamo Navy Base. Airliners were hijacked. A hijacked Cuban Viscount crashed into Nipe Bay, killing 58 people, including Americans. Assassinations were commonplace. Policemen, soldiers, and government employees were killed.

The Cuban government responded and terror was met with counterterror. A revolution was born. A small number of men and women had succeeded; they had made a revolution.

The revolution was successful and on January 1, 1959 Castro came to power. Almost immediately he began to export revolution throughout Latin America. He started with the invasion of the Dominican Republic on June 12, 1959, which failed. He tried to work with the communist parties in Latin America but was rebuffed because they were no longer revolutionary. The communist leaders had joined their parties in the early 1930's, and after thirty years had attained a sound political reputation. They had arrived at a *modus vivendi* with local governments and security officials who tolerated them if they did not make trouble. A few party leaders were willing to give up their status quo for a risky chance at revolution. Two who did were Carlos Marighella and Camara Ferreira, both of whom bolted the Brazilian Communist Party for urban terrorism. Other Latin American communist leaders could not, however, reject Castro's proposals for revolution outright. To have done so would have destroyed their revolutionary credentials. Instead they hedged. They spoke in favor of revolution but added that the time was not propitious for revolution. They argued that their government was too strong, the army too well prepared. The party leaders gave the excuse that they needed more time to recruit, train, and equip men. Only then would the time be ripe for revolution.

Castro had been confronted with an identical situation in Cuba, and knew he had to force the situation for it to become ripe for revolution. He and his military planners—his brother, Raul, and

Ernesto "Che" Guevara—formalized the doctrine of the Cuban revolution: "Revolution makes the revolution."

Their experiences in the Sierra Maestra Mountains evolved into a new concept of guerrilla warfare. The basic military unit of the Sierra Maestra campaign, the column, became a mobile strike column operating from a fixed base. This was an innovation in guerrilla warfare. In Cuba the sanctuary was the Sierra Maestra Mountains, but to make the theory adaptable for export to other countries, the sanctuary was established on one side of an international boundary. This permitted a mobile strike column to cross the international boundary and attack the enemy. After the attack the strike column retreated to its sanctuary knowing that the pursuing army was prohibited by law from following them across the international frontier.

Communist leaders in Latin America were not only highly skeptical of mobile strike columns and revolution through terrorist tactics, but were very outspoken in their criticism. The Cuban concept was in direct opposition to the long accepted communist doctrine that revolution came from action by the masses.

Guevara and the Bolivian Experiment

During the heat of the controversy, Che Guevara volunteered to clandestinely enter Bolivia and create the conditions for revolution. He had carefully selected Bolivia as the test area because the international boundaries of Brazil, Paraguay, Argentina, and Bolivia all converged. Although sparsely settled, the Eastern Andean slopes contain a large enough population to support a revolutionary action base.

Guevara's plan was a simple yet innovative one. He planned to organize a strike column in Bolivia and then strike into Brazil. Afterwards he would retreat back into Bolivia, leaving any pursuing Brazilian force stopped at the frontier. On the next attack Guevara could strike into Bolivia itself and retreat into the remote frontier area of Paraguay. This would be repeated until the area was in turmoil. The countries attacked would eventually respond with counterterrorism actions and soon a revolutionary situation would exist. Then the strike column would exploit the revolutionary situation to recruit new guerrillas.

Guevara failed in his mission. He was unable to organize a strike column in Bolivia, not because the concept was invalid, but because the communist party of Bolivia refused to help him. Guevara also failed because of well-organized and executed counterterrorist tactics of the Bolivian Army. They did not give Guevara the time nor the opportunity to organize. From the time he was discovered in Bolivia, the Bolivian Army pursued him relentlessly. He was unable to stop to rest or organize. He was forced to keep running. Unknowingly, Guevara turned into a blind canyon while retreating.

He was captured at Quebrada del Yuro ravine by Captain Gary Prado of the Bolivian Rangers. Che was taken and imprisoned in the schoolhouse in La Higuera.

While waiting to be executed, Guevara was asked a number of questions about Cuba and about himself. He was willing to talk because he was not being interrogated and it helped pass the time. Ironically, one of the questions concerned the number of executions in Cuba since Castro rose to power. He contested the number which was cited and replied, "That's greatly exaggerated! About 1,500, no more than 1,800 were killed. That's all. Of course, that doesn't include guerrillas. We executed every guerrilla we captured."

As soon as he said it he knew it was a slip and he smiled. The conversation continued. Minutes later he was executed. His last words were, *'Acuerdate que se esta matando un hombre,'* "Remember, you are killing a man."

Che's family carried on his tradition. His sister Ana Maria Guevara is married to Fernando Luis Alvarez, reported to be the chief of the JRC Headquarters in Paris. Alvarez uses the pseudonym "Pelado." Che's brother Roberto is a member of the JRC and reportedly went on a mission for Fidel Castro in Luanda, Angola in 1977.

Origins of the "Foco" Theory

The concept of the mobile strike column remained dormant until the late 1970's when Cuba sent large troop movements into Africa. With their arrival the strike columns theory became the strategy of the Cuban-supported national liberation movements in Africa. The new Cuba plan for urban terrorism developed along different lines. It became the "Foco" theory.

Foco is a Spanish word meaning the center or headquarters of a rural or urban guerrilla movement. Italian and French terrorists using the Foco theory have changed "foco" to "nuclei." For example, a terrorist group in Paris is the Armed Nuclei for Peoples' Autonomy (NPAP). In the United States the Weathermen used the Foco theory, and in their publications described it as follows:

"It is not necessary to organize the population as a whole to accomplish a revolution. A small group of insurgents can act as a voice for the discontented elements to channel all of their energy into the defeat of the government."

The Foco theory is the core of the urban terrorism that prevails today in Italy, Germany, and elsewhere. According to the Foco theory, if a revolutionary leader wants to lead a revolt against the government, he does not wait for the conditions to be ripe for revolution. He starts his own revolution. As the Weathermen published in their book *Prairie Fire,*

". . . the duty of a revolutionary is to make the revolution."

The Foco theory changed terrorism from the execution of random acts of terror to a series of planned acts of terrorism intended to destroy a government. Terror changed from a tactic to a form of revolution.

Marighella and Foco

Carlos Marighella, a Marxist philosopher, continued to develop the Foco theory. A long time communist, he was a man of considerable intelligence who was once an engineering student in Recife, Brazil. At the end of the Brazilian revolution in 1964, he was arrested by the police in a movie theatre in Rio de Janeiro. The police surrounded the area where he was seated, the theater was lighted, and the police advanced on Marighella with drawn guns. He was taken by surprise, and shouted an obscenity as he charged toward the police. The police fired to stop him. No one expected an act of such desperation and rage. Marighella was taken to a hospital where he was treated and put in a guarded room to recuperate. But he spoke such profane diatribes against the government that he was removed to an isolated prison cell.

Marighella disagreed with the non-revolutionary leadership of the pro-Soviet Brazilian Communist Party. He wanted a revolution and he wanted it right now. He went to Cuba in 1967 to attend the Organization of Latin American Solidarity. Marighella talked with Castro and was convinced he was right by what he saw and heard. He returned to Brazil and broke with the orthodox communist leaders. Marighella left Rio de Janeiro and went to Sao Paulo where he took over its Communist Party machinery and organized terror gangs. He formed the Revolutionary Communist Party of Brazil and the Action for National Liberation (ALN).

One of Marighella's victims was a young U.S. Army captain, Charles Chandler. Chandler had just completed a tour of duty in Vietnam and was sent to Brazil to learn Portuguese prior to a teaching assignment at West Point. He was a highly motivated young man who lectured to university students on the righteousness of the United States' cause in Southeast Asia. He was a high profile personality and came to the attention of the terrorists.

Marighella's men cased Chandler's residence and learned that every Saturday morning Chandler drove his wife and children shopping. They also learned that Chandler, like most Americans in Sao Paulo, lived in a small house with a garage in back. The driveway between the house and the outside wall was so narrow that the car doors could only be opened in the garage or in the street. Passengers could be let out only in the garage or on the front walk where Chandler always picked up his family.

On a fateful Saturday morning, Chandler began to back his car out of the driveway when three terrorists raced from across the street, where they had been waiting. They fired automatic weapons into the rear of his car. Caught between the house and the outside wall, Chandler could not open the car doors to escape. He was killed defenselessly in a perfect trap. The ALN left pamphlets behind stating "Brazil is the Vietnam of America."

Several months later, on November 4, 1969, the police caught Marighella in an ambush in Sao Paulo. He fought back and was killed at the age of 58.

Marighella became a hero to terrorists, but even more importantly he left behind a legacy to advance the Foco theory of terrorism. He wrote the *Mini-Manual of the Urban Guerrilla,* a handbook on how to be an urban terrorist. The book was translated into many languages, printed in Havana, and distributed worldwide. I have seen the mini-manual throughout Latin America as well as in Iran, printed in Farsi, and in Turkey, printed in Turkish. The mini-manual is highly regarded by the Red Brigades of Italy and is considered by them "the best book ever written on urban terrorism." It was used by the Symbionese Liberation Army on the West coast. Patty Hearst took the name "Tania" from Che's girlfriend in Bolivia. The Foco theory became international.

Marighella was the first to try to use Che Guevara's Foco concept in the cities—not the rural areas. After his failure he was criticized by proponents of urban guerrilla warfare because Marighella had stated he viewed the war in the city as "tactical," leading the warfare in the rural area where it would become "strategic." Abraham Guillen, a proponent of warfare in the city, maintained Marighella committed a fundamental mistake in concept.

A dual use of the word "Foco" has come into being: one is the name of the initial guerrilla organization, which became the name of a theory of guerrilla warfare.

The Foco theory had a predictable reaction in the communist world. The Soviets said nothing. A few Soviet diplomats denounced terrorism, but counterterrorists commented that publicly the Soviets could do nothing else. It was disputed by the communists that Marxist-Leninist revolutionaries would wage a revolution without the backing and the support of the local communist party. The Foco theory has still not been accepted by the orthodox communist parties.

The Chinese communists rejected the Foco theory. Guevara's death in Bolivia and the failure of urban terrorists in Venezuela and the Dominican Republic are pointed out to students as "romantic adventurism" in the guerrilla training center at Nanking.

The Chinese-Foco Conflict

The Foco theory conflicts with the principles of guerrilla warfare which the Chinese have developed over the past forty years. To give credence to a theory as innovative and untested as the Foco theory is a put-down of the Chinese in a field in which they consider themselves expert.

The Chinese fundamental precept of guerrilla warfare requires the organization of a people's army which rises and forms in the area where the enemy will be fought. It does not fight foreign wars. It fights at home in the area it knows best.

A Chinese-trained guerrilla leader told me during the Vietnam conflict: "The United States can never win in Vietnam. Never, never, not in a hundred years. Because your soldiers are alien to the soil."

The Chinese guerrilla army rises from the people. It starts when two men join together to fight the enemy. Two men are strong enough to kill one armed man for his weapon. With that weapon they can kill another armed man, then have two weapons, and can recruit another man to join their growing army. A growing army does not have to be supplied with weapons. They will find their own. The people's army increases in size and attacks smaller government forces. The government counterattacks in strength and the people's army disperses and flows back into the population and disappears. When the danger is over the people's army re-forms and then disperses when necessary only to form again. The guerrilla army becomes bigger and joins with another growing army and whole regions fall under guerrilla control. Cities are surrounded and isolated by the encircling guerrilla army. Lines of supply and communications fall under guerrilla control. Slowly the cities are choked to death. The process of strangulation is never hurried. Chinese terrorists do not penetrate the city defenses to speed the demise through acts of terror, because the Chinese consider terrorist attacks inside the enemy's stronghold to be foolhardy. Guerrilla sympathizers in the cities are directed by the guerrilla leaders to engage only in the amount of opposition which is possible without imprisonment or execution.

The only time the Chinese guerrillas engaged in urban terrorism was in Vietnam. It was justified because of the presence of a superpower, the United States. A Chinese guerrilla army in an ordinary situation inflicts casualties continuously upon the enemy forces. The object is not to hold ground but to kill the enemy to the point where the enemy force can no longer replace its losses. When this point is reached, the enemy is destroyed.

In Vietnam the guerrilla forces could not bleed the enemy to death because of the United States, with its large population, was able to replace losses in combat zones. The United States had, in fact, over a half million troops in Vietnam. Not only were losses replaced, but the United States had more troops in the combat zone than the guerrilla forces could handle. As a means to equalize the enemy's troop strength, the Vietnamese sent terrorists into the cities. But unlike the Foco theory which is to terrorize the populace, the Vietnamese terrorists were targeted against government and military installations and personnel. The people and the means of production were spared. The strategy was successful. American and South Vietnamese troops were withdrawn from the combat zones and stationed in the cities to defend against further terrorist attacks.

Considering the successes of the Chinese guerrilla armies, it was logical for the Chinese to view the Foco theory, and the mobile strike columns operating from a fixed base, with skepticism.

The Guillen Doctrine

During the early 1960's Abraham Guillen, a Spanish Marxist and author, was exiled in Uruguay. He tried to convince the Cuban revolutionary leaders there that the guerrilla forces should be located in the cities and not in the rural areas. Guillen also maintained that the impetus for revolution should be in the cities and not the countryside. The cities provided better protection and cover from the enemy's superior artillery and air force, he argued. The enemy was not going to destroy its own cities to capture or kill the terrorists. The Cubans, however, believed in the concept of the mobile strike column operating from a fixed base, and Che Guevara rejected Guillen's argument. Guevara believed the three fundamental lessons the revolutionaries learned from the Cuban Revolution were:

1. Popular forces can win a war against the enemy.
2. It is not necessary to wait until all of the conditions for making a revolution exist; the insurrection can create them.
3. In underdeveloped Latin America the countryside is the basic area for fighting.

Academic substance was added to the Cuban concept through the previous writings of Herbert Marcuse, a German Marxist who fled Germany prior to World War II. Marcuse settled in the United States and worked for United States Intelligence during WWII. He believed that a revolution had to be made by revolutionaries because the proletariat had become a part of the establishment and had lost its zeal, even its desire, to foment a revolution. Secondly, Marcuse condoned violence. He wrote, "If they (revolutionaries) use violence, they do not start a new chain of violence, but try to break an established one" meaning that since the establishment engages in violence, it is not violent for a revolutionary to use violence for the revolution.

Believing that the rural theory was the right theory, Guevara embarked upon his ill-fated Bolivian venture. After the defeat of Guevara in Bolivia, Guillen witnessed the destruction of the Tupamaros by the Uruguayan military and police forces. The Tupamaros were defeated because they lived in organizational safehouses and the domino theory applied. The capture and arrest of one led to another and then another Tupamaro. Guillen then combined the concepts of the Chinese Peoples' Army with the Cuban Foco theory. He wrote that the urban guerrilla army should rise from the city's populace in the same manner as the Chinese People's army rises from the countryside. He advocated that the urban guerrilla forces disperse when attacked, hide in the population from which it came, then regroup and enlarge to hit the enemy with greater force. Guillen insisted that the Tupamaros should not run their operations from organizational safehouses, which he termed "fixed bases." Instead, he urged that the urban guerrilla live in their own homes and come together only to carry out a mission.

Guillen also urged that each urban guerilla group be self-directed. A guerrilla group should not be dependent upon a central command structure because arrested members of a central command are likely to reveal the identity of subordinate members when subjected to interrogation.

Few terrorist organizations have been able to apply Guillen's theories. His doctrine that urban guerrillas live apart and come together only to fight is difficult to implement. The need for security and clandestineness precludes leading normal lives. Operating clandestinely, it may take days to plan one brief meeting with another terrorist. A casing may take several weeks. In order not to be conspicuous, a great deal of the terrorists' work must be done during regular working hours so that the terrorist can blend in with people living normal lives. They must account to their family and friends for their absences, their lack of steady employment, and their source of money. Because of these pressures and questions most terrorists leave home and settle into an organizational safehouse. They try to blend into the scene, but as Guillen pointed out, they become vulnerable. An informer living in the area is able to spot the terrorist: a person living comfortably with no visible signs of income and no fixed routine.

This problem has affected a number of terrorist organizations. The Baader-Meinhoff gang did not move into a safehouse unless it was an upper middle class type of dwelling. "Carlos" lived in the best hotels. His preference ran to the Hilton hotels. The Red Brigades, in trying to cope with the problem, issued a pamphlet with rules on how to merge into the area and not be noticed. Those living in safehouses were to maintain the premises, put up curtains, keep radios and phonographs turned down low, and in general stay out of the landlord's way.

Other groups, such as the Weather Underground in the United States, were able to successfully apply Guillen's theory for the descentralization of command. Their publication *Punch With The Red Army* states ". . . . but there is no such thing as a cell without its initiative. For this reason it is essential to avoid any rigidity in the organization in order to permit the greatest possible initiative on the part of the cell. The old type hierarchy of the traditional left doesn't exist in our organization.

"This means that, except for the priority of objectives set by the strategic command, any cell can decide to assault a bank, to kidnap or to execute an agent of the government, a figure identified with reaction, a spy or informer, a major heroin distributor, and carry out any kind of propaganda or war of nerves against the enemy without the need to consult the general command.

"No cell can remain inactive waiting for orders from above. Its obligation is to act."

Note: For a listing and classification of terrorist organizations, see Appendix.

4

Worldwide Terror

International terrorism constitutes many spectacular acts of violence, and it is intended to do so. From 1969–78, 2,662 people were taken hostage by international terrorists, another 1,015 were injured, and 620 were killed. These statistics do not take into account internal terrorism which goes on day after day, taking an enormous loss of life and causing the downfall of governments.

Internal terrorism seldom becomes worldwide headline news. When it does, it is because the brutality of the act commands headlines. The attack on Kolwezi in Zaire, where countless civilians were butchered, was that kind of terrorism. The brutality was of such a degree that it threatened the economic base of Zaire and the ability of the government to survive. Kolwezi was brilliantly and faultlessly executed, and there have been similar terrorists acts.

On the evening of June 23, 1978, eight or more guerrillas seized the Elim Pentecostal Mission station in the Vambu Mountains of Rhodesia. They robbed the school and herded the 250 students together. While lecturing them on the evils of the white man, they brutally massacred the seven white staff members and their five children in front of the students. The whites were executed to terrorize the 250 black students who then were sent to their homes where they told in vivid detail what they had seen.

Terrorism and Patron Governments

The fact is, during the last quarter of the twentieth century, terror has become a form of revolution supported by governments to win political victories. These governments include almost all of Africa, most of the Mideast, and some Western and Asian countries. These governments support terrorists with money, supplies, weapons, and even false documentation. These "patron states" of terrorism are authoritarian dictatorships, communist countries or a combination of both. They export terror to strengthen their own revolutionary credentials and to advance their own political objectives. In other words, patron states export terror to countries where the patron states want a change of government.

The most active patron states are in the Mideast and North Africa. The leader is Libya, led by Libyan Chief of State, Colonel Muammar Qaddafi. Qaddafi publicly opposes terrorism but maintains that freedom fighters are not terrorists and have the prerogative to fight by whatever means they find appropriate. Over twenty terrorist training camps have been verified in Libya and many more are thought to exist.

Iraq, another "patron state," supports three kinds of terror. They are terror attacks against Israel, terror attacks against Syria, and terror attacks against any moderate state which would participate in peace talks with Israel.

While the People's Democratic Republic of Yemen (PDRY) lacks substantial financial resources, it does not lack revolutionary zeal. It provides terrorist training facilities, safehavens, and encouragement to terrorists and would-be terrorists. A well-known Wadi Haddad Palestinian training camp in Yemen trains internal and international terrorists from Germany, Sweden, Lebanon, and the United States. In the training camp there is no distinction between international and internal terrorists.

Algeria has consistently given support to terrorists. The Algerian Government has provided safehavens for terrorists such as "Carlos," Abu Daud, and the Japanese Red Army terrorists. Algeria also uses its diplomatic pouch, as does Libya, in support of terrorism. It was suspected by Brazilian authorities that the machine guns used to assassinate Charles Chandler in Sao Paulo were brought into Brazil through Algerian diplomats.

In sub-Sahara Africa the patron states are Uganda, Somalia, and Tanzania. In Uganda, infamous Idi Amin maintained a vehement anti-Israeli posture, aggravated considerably by the Entebbe rescue, and kept close ties with Libya and Iraq. He regarded the Palestinians as "fellow Muslims." Somalia has given aid to Palestinians, while Tanzania has supported Cuban-instructed liberation movements.

The patron state of terror in Latin America is Cuba, whose foreign policy is to export revolution and terror to all parts of the world. The export of revolution has been the official policy of Cuba since 1959. Five successive United States administrations have tried to induce a change in Cuba's policy, but none have succeeded. Castro refuses to modify his revolutionary policy. In the Kolwezi attack Cuba advisors accompanied the attacking columns to their infiltration point into Zambia.

In Asia the two patron states were North Korea and the People's Republic of China. North Korea aids conventional revolutionary groups. However, conventional revolutionary groups contain terrorists.

The People's Republic of China states categorically that it rejects terrorism but it supports Palestinian groups which use terrorism.

The Soviet Union has two priority missions in the field of terrorism. It supports wars of liberation, especially in Africa, where terror is a major tactical and strategic weapon. Clearly, another Russian priority is to support internal revolutionary groups which threaten non-Marxist governments. It is in wars of national liberation and internal revolution that major political victories can be won. The position of the Soviet Union was succinctly stated by *Izvestiya* on March 30, 1976.

". . . the Soviet Union is opposed to acts of terrorism which disrupt the diplomatic activities of states and their representatives, transport communications between them and the normal course of international contacts and meetings. It is quite inadmissible to extend the concept of international terrorism to the national liberation struggle, to actions offering resistance to an aggressor on territories occupied by him and to working people's demonstrations for their rights against oppression by exploiters." International terrorism is a poor third in priority to the Soviets, ranking below the wars of national liberation and internal terror.

This statement means that for the public record, the Soviets do not approve of terrorist seizure of embassies or the holding of diplomats as hostages. The Soviets are opposed to hijacking and to incidents such as the seizure of the OPEC offices in Vienna by "Carlos." The common thread which runs throughout all terrorist acts opposed by the Soviets is a similarity to tactics which could also threaten the

Soviets. These tactics have caused incidents in countries occupied by the Soviets. Of greatest importance, however, is the Soviet admission of support for insurgents who practice terrorism. Thc Sovicts admit they will continue to support revolutionary groups, national liberation movements and workers' organizations which use terrorism to attain their goals. To the Soviets this is not terrorism but part of the international political struggle, and they will continue to support such organizations as the Turkish Liberation Army, the People's Sacrifice Guerrillas, the Irish Republican Army and any other Marxist revolutionary group.

In 1977 alone, the Soviets exported 3.3 billion dollars in arms to the third world, mostly radical Arab states such as Algeria, Libya, and Syria.

International terrorist groups are Marxist-Leninist in political orientation. Some communist parties members would oppose terrorism but they cannot. Why? Because they cannot deny that the Soviets aid and abet terrorism on the theory that there are many different roads to world socialism. One road is through legitimate political parties. There are many countries, such as Italy, where the communist party takes part in the electoral and parliamentary processes. But the other road is through revolution by terrorists, and the two roads are traveled simultaneously.

The Cuba-Africa Connection

Turning to the geographic areas in conflict, Africa is rampant with terrorism which is international in nature. But because it is associated with national liberation movements, the United States government does not intervene to help those under attack. Cuba, on the other hand, is actively involved in training, instructing, and directly assisting national liberation movements. A reasonable estimate puts over 50,000 Cubans in Africa, making up a military force of instructors, soldiers, and pilots. There are 20,000 to 25,000 Cubans in Angola; 1,000 in the Congo; 15,000 in Ethiopia; 500 in Tanzania; 1,000 in Guinea; and 200 in Sierra Leone. The Cubans brought with them the Cuban concept of rural guerrilla warfare, teaching national liberation movements how to use mobile guerrilla columns to operate from a fixed base inside a sanctuary, such as Zambia or Mozambique, and to conduct raids attacking hostile targets in another country, like Rhodesia.

The Kolwezi attack provides an example of the Cuban concept of regional guerrilla warfare and the use of terror. About 2,000 guerrillas from Angola crossed Zambia into Shaba Province where they rendezvoused at pre-selected locations. It was estimated the infiltration process took about a month. Once reassembled the guerrillas formed into two columns and went on to attack and terrorize Kolwezi. When confronted by a European military force, they retreated back into their sanctuary.

By all indications, the present pattern of warfare will continue in Africa. A guerrilla-terrorist situation cannot be reversed unless a counterforce is created. So long as the Soviets and Cubans expend military resources in Africa the situation will deteriorate. There is no reason for optimism south of the Sahara.

Terror in Latin America

The situation in Latin America continues to fluctuate as it has for the past twenty years. Twenty years ago the Caribbean and Central America were troubled areas. Ten years ago Brazil, Uruguay, and Argentina were deeply troubled by urban terrorists, but through the effective use of counterterrorist tactics, the threat was removed. Now Central America is again troubled as it was twenty years ago. Terrorism is on the rise in Guatemala, El Salvador, and Honduras.

In Guatemala there has been terrorist cruelty as well as cruelty by the counterterrorists. In one case in Guatemala, a small businessman called on the chief of a security unit and reported he had been approached by two terrorists to use his house to store arms. The police chief demanded that the businessman repeat his story. When he did, the security chief drew his revolver and shot and killed the man. The security chief thought that anyone whom the terrorists would approach for help must be of similar anti-government orientation, or the terrorists never would have approached him. This was no way to run a counterterrorist operation. It turned off the critically needed flow of intelligence. When people refuse to cooperate with the government, the government is in jeopardy.

In anguish a Guatemalan journalist wrote: "In Guatemala each sees violence from his own perspective. Students protest over violence against students, officials, over the deaths of their agents, and even we of the press complain with special intensity over attacks on our own colleagues. This is not a new phenomenon. Blood begets blood, hate brings vengeance, and these ingredients are poisoning the soul of our nation, perhaps irreparably."

Insurgency in El Salvador

By the end of 1979 El Salvador reached the penultimate stage of Cuban-directed insurgency which had racked the country for several years. El Salvador supported more violence per square foot of land than any country in the world, and terrorist targets could survive only by using and practicing total concepts of security.

One dramatic example illustrating the need for total security took place in November 1979. Terrorists drove to the victim's home, which was protected by conventional anti-burglar devices, and parked their Chevrolet van on the sidewalk alongside the brick wall surrounding the perimeter of the victim's property. Using the roof of the van, they scaled over the wall and its barbed wire apron. As is so often the case in internal terrorism, the bodyguards, seeing the flagrant breach of the perimeter defenses, fled without firing a shot. Unmolested, the terrorists crossed the lawn carrying large sledge hammers which they used to break through the next defense, the house itself.

Wielding the sledge hammers, they began smashing through the protective iron bars, doors and locks. As always when insurgency is in its final stages, there was no police response. Finally the large front door gave way and the terrorists prepared to enter and kidnap their victim.

Meanwhile, the victim inside was alerted. He had his choice between an automatic pistol and a submachine gun. Unfortunately, he chose the pistol. He took a position, covering the front door, and when the first terrorist entered, he fired and the terrorist fell. The second terrorist entered, and he, too, was hit. The victim did not have the firepower to cope with the entire attacking force, and a terrorist's bullet hit him in the leg. He collapsed and the terrorists entered, seized him by the legs and began to drag him out of the room. The victim's wife appeared with the submachine gun and pointed it at the terrorists and tried to fire. The terrorists saw that she did not know how to function the safety, took the gun away from her and dragged the victim to the waiting van.

Under ordinary circumstances, the victim's security was adequate. His perimeter was protected. He employed bodyguards and his house had most of the recommended security devices including iron bars, a sturdy door and security alarm. All to no avail.

In this case, the victim needed a submachine gun or automatic shotgun to bring down as many of his attackers as quickly as possible. He then needed an interior bullet-proof saferoom to which he and his family could retreat. Saferooms can be further strengthened through the installation of gas ducts from which tear gas and nausea gas can be sprayed against anyone who tries to approach the room. These are but a few of the measures taken for complete security.

More conventional kidnap cases take place with great frequency in Salvador. One such case involved two Americans, Dennis McDonald and Fausto Buchelli, who were kidnapped in September 1979. The case began to unfold when McDonald and his chauffeur drove Buchelli, who was visiting from McDonald's home office, to the airport. As they drove along the highway, a small vehicle with two men inside pulled into a trailing position in back of McDonald's car. A small, open-bed truck, carrying a number of men and women, pulled out of a side road and took a position in front of McDonald's car. The jaws of the trap were in place.

Whenever McDonald's chauffeur tried to pass the truck, the truck driver jockeyed to the left, obstructing McDonald's car. Suddenly, when the truck driver reached a previously selected site on the highway, he slammed on the brakes, bringing the truck to an almost immediate stop. McDonald's car smashed into the truck's rear while simultaneously the trailing car deliberately drove into the rear of McDonald's car, sandwiching it with such impact that the doors sprung open. The terrorists jumped out of the truck. They were masked and armed. McDonald, Buchelli and the chauffeur were pulled from their car. The chauffeur was killed and the two Americans were taken away forcibly as hostages.

Several days after the kidnapping, a group calling itself the Partido Obrero Revolutionario de America Central (PORAC-Central American Revolutionary Workers Party) claimed responsibility for the act. Yet from an analysis of the modus operandi it appeared the terrorist organization which carried out the kidnapping was actually the Ejercito Revolucionario del Pueblo (ERP-People's Revolutionary Army). This tentative identification was made on the basis of previous terrorist acts committed by the ERP. The ERP has always used violence. Its members wore masks while committing a terrorist act. A large number of ERP militants were always involved in a single act. After the act was committed a front organization, such as the PORAC, claimed responsiblity. Everything seemed to match.

The ERP is not the only terrorist organization in El Salvador. There are four revolutionary terrorist organizations active in El Salvador and by all criteria each should be classifed as an international terrorist organization because each has struck out and attacked international targets. They are 1) Fuerzas Popular de Liberation (FPL—Popular Liberation Forces), 2) Fuerzas Popular de Liberation Farabundo Marti (FPL/FM—Farabundo Marti Popular Liberation Forces, 3) Fuerzas Armada de Resistencia National (FARN—Armed Forces of National Resistance, and 4) ERP.

Of the four groups the FPL/FM is the largest and most active. For all practical purposes it is Cuban-directed. Its leadership cannot pursue objectives counter to the desires of the Cuban intelligence service (DGI). It's ideological and political orientation is Marxist and violently anti-American.

The FPL/FM has a remarkable record of success. It is believed that every one of its actions which reached the implementation stage were successful and that not one of its top leaders has ever been captured by the police. This perhaps is not a difficult feat in the present environment. The Salvadorean government is virtually without information or intelligence on terrorist activities. Money is budgeted for this purpose but it is siphoned off and pocketed at the top, never reaching the intelligence and security echelons whose job it is to combat terrorism. The only tool left to them is the interrogation of captured terrorists to obtain operational leads, but this has brought charges of brutality and torture. Consequently, rather than face charges of human rights violations, the police have killed captives to prevent just or unjust allegations of mistreatment.

Nevertheless, the FPL/FM and the other terrorist organizations in El Salvador have perfected kidnapping to the extent that it is now one of the biggest businesses in the country, perhaps outranked only by coffee. Ransoms run in the neighborhood of one to ten million dollars per victim. Terrorist organizations have become so wealthy that they now hire members of the middle class to handle terrorist administrative and organizational tasks at twice the salaries they received in the private sector. Other innovations have also developed in the art of kidnapping. For instance, in El Salvador the terrorists ask the kidnap victim to ingest three daily doses of Valium No. 5 to eliminate his fear and discomfort during the ransom negotiations. The Valium makes guarding the victim much easier and lessens the possibility of escape.

Similar to the other terrorist organizations in El Salvador, the FPL/FM controls a popular front group, the Bloque Popular Revolucionario (BPR—Popular Revolutionary Bloc) which is leftist oriented. The fact that these popular fronts actually exist and are on the rampage in El Salvador is somewhat unusual. The control of a front group is the goal of any insurgent group. It can then direct the front to protest, mount disturbances, strike and riot while the insurgents conduct terrorist and military actions in support of the front groups.

In most cases, the government in power uses the maximum force possible to prevent mob-related chaos and destruction. This is not so in El Salvador. The four front groups there openly engage in sabotage, the illegal occupation of buildings and even hostage taking. Such was the case with Deborah Loff, an American Peace Corps volunteer, who was kidnapped by the February 28 Popular League on December 19, 1979. Fortunately, Loff was safely released in early 1980.

On November 2, 1979 the FPL/FM issued a communique announcing it activated a new terrorist organization, the Ejercito del Pueblo de Liberacion (EPL, People's Liberation Army). The communique said the EPL was baptized into combat on November first when it attacked the National Telecommunications Administration warehouse and engaged in a ten minute firefight.

The second most active terrorist group in El Salvador is the FARN. It is of Marxist orientation and also follows the directional lines of the Soviet Union and Cuba. It maintains ties with Cuba and the USSR. Many of its members were trained in guerrilla camps in Guatemala. The FARN maintains a front group, the Frente de Accion Unificado (FAPU—Unified Popular Action Front).

The ERP is one of the smaller, albeit active, terrorist groups. Some Salvadoreans believe it is not a separate group but the action arm of the larger but seemingly dormant FPL. But it is the ERP which directs the front group, Ligas Popular 28 Febrero (LP Febrero—February 28 Popular Leagues, which takes its name from the day in 1977 when more than 100 people were shot in the main city plaza during a demonstration).

Salvadorean businesses and other potential targets of terrorist acts have armed themselves and taken other security precautions in their attempt to survive and carry on their business activities. Wives and children have been sent out of the country to the United States and Europe. The husbands who stay behind carry .45 caliber automatics everywhere, loaded and cocked with the safety on. The automatic is carried inside the belt or placed within easy reach. Vehicles, generally of the four wheel drive type, are armored and travel in convoys of three cars with bodyguards in the first and third, the potential target in the center car. Once enroute the convoys do not stop for traffic signals or red lights but keep moving at rapid speed until the destination is reached. Routes are varied. Routines are altered. Most people stay home at night, but some security-conscious businessmen have found it best to move around at night. The darkness is an impediment to the terrorist in planning an ambush and in making certain the right person is attacked.

However, with the breakdown of police protection and the heavy firepower possessed by the terrorists, even armored convoys with as many as six to eight bodyguards are sometimes not enough. A wealthy, well-liked Salvadorean businessman, Roberto Poma, was kidnapped and his six armed bodyguards killed in the ambush. His family paid $2 million in ransom, and the Salvadorean government released Ana Guadalupe Martinez, an ERP leader, from jail. Only the terrorists knew that Poma had died in the initial ambush. After the ransom was met, Poma's lifeless body was recovered.

Ernesto Liebes, a wealthy Salvadorean businesman, was riding in an armored car driven by his chauffeur/bodyguard when their car was involved in a minor collision, apparently staged by terrorists. The chauffeur stopped the car and got out to inspect the damage—a definite security violation—and left the door unlocked. Armed terrorists descended upon the vehicle, opened the door and took Liebes hostage. They demanded $10 million ransom, but apparently, in accord with instructions left to them by the victim, the family refused to pay. Liebes' body was subsequently recovered.

The Salvadorean business community and the country's non-communist population believe that Salvador's end is near. That is unless the United States government assists in combatting these terrorists, who receive unlimited support from Cuba and through Cuba from the Soviet Union. The United States government, too, is aware that Cuba may soon be the dominant force in El Salvador and Central America. In accord with the present policy of trying to mollify revolutionary groups, the United States is trying to convince the Salvadorean government to ease controls and adapt policies to accommodate the dissidents. Most of the business community and the noncommunists are fearful of U.S. policy and charge that the United States is trying to enforce its policy through economic pressure. Consequently, the economic situation in El Salvador is bleak. The Salvadoreans say that the United States wants to affect the type of change in El Salvador that it did in Nicaragua, but the two countries are vastly different.

The difference in El Salvador is the lack of a sizeable middle class as there was in Nicaragua. In the Nicaraguan insurgency, a part of the middle class sided with the insurgents against the government. The United States believed this part of society—the merchants, businessmen and other professionals—could temper the communist revolutionaries and mold them into a government of Western orientation.

El Salvador is not made up of the same social composition as Nicaragua. The social make-up of the country is unique. It is composed of an upper middle class and an upper class below which there is only the working class and the poor. In other words, the entire productive class is pitted against the insurgents. There is no group in between to work with the communists and temper their policies.

It probably makes little difference. El Salvador is falling to the insurgents and it is doubtful that they will compromise while they are winning. A total victory will probably be theirs.

Colombia and Venezuela

At the Northern Tier of Latin America, in Venezuela and particularly Colombia, the guerrilla situation remains the same. Ironicaly both Venezuela and Colombia are South America's strongest democracies, but Bogota is also the kidnap capital of the world, with 84 kidnapping during 1977.

The pro-Soviet Revolutionary Armed Forces of Colombia, (FARC) with 1,000 men, holds large areas of the country. American citizens are held prisoners by guerrilla forces in Venezuela and Colombia. Barring some unforeseen development, the situation in Venezuela and Colombia will remain stalemated.

Palestinian Terrorists

It is imperative to discuss, if only in summary, the Palestinian terrorist organizations. The largest group represented in the Palestine Liberation Organization (PLO). The overall political umbrella organization of the Palestinians is Al Fatah. Outwardly, Al Fatah represents the moderate position of the PLO but covertly it unleashes the Black September Organization (BSO) to execute its acts of terrorism. Al Fatah leaders are Yasir Arafat who uses the war name "Abu Amar," Salah Khalaf, "Abu Iyad," and the BSO leader, Khalil Faris al Wazir, "Abu Jihad." Tactically, Al Fatah has used a two-pronged offensive. It ran cross-border military operations into Israel from bases inside Lebanon. These bases are located in southeast Lebanon in the Urqub region known as "Fatahland." Israel retaliated against cross-border raids with military incursions into Lebanon to destroy Fatah military bases. In the military and political turmoil the delicately balanced Lebanese government of Christians and Muslims broke apart. In April 1975 the Lebanese civil war began.

The other prong of Al Fatah is the covert effort of the BSO. This action since 1971 has included the following acts of terror:

1. Assassination of Jordanian Prime Minister Wasfi al Tal in November 1971.
2. Five Jordanians assassinated in West Germany, February 1972.
3. Munich Olympic Massacre, September 1972.
4. Seizure of the Israeli Embassy in Bangkok.
5. Murder of two American diplomats during seizure of Saudi Arabian Embassy in Khartoum, March 1973.

After the end of the 1973 war the Fatah changed its immediate perspective and announced it sought limited territorial goals in Israel, specifically the return of the West Bank and Gaza, and was willing to sit down and discuss a peace settlement with Israel representatives. This caused a splintering of the Palestinians and the Rejection Front was formed. Foremost among the terror organizations of the Rejection Front, as well as its founder, is the Marxist Popular Front for the Liberation of Palestine (PFLP). Its political goal is to free all of Palestine, destroy Israel, and establish a Marxist state. It aspires to do this through terrorism. The leader of the PFLP is George Haffash while the master planner of PFLP terror operations was the late Wadi Haddad. Both the Japanese Red Army and Ilich Ramirez Sanchez, "Carlos," are allied with the PFLP. "Carlos" was, in fact, identified as a member of the PFLP taking orders from Wadi Haddad.

The following are the significant terror actions of the PFLP:

1. Four European and U.S. airlines were hijacked and then destroyed in Jordan, September 1970.
2. Lod Airport massacre (executed by the Japanese Red Army with planning and support of the PFLP), May 1972.
3. Hijacking of Japan Air Lines jet enroute to Dubai (with Japanese Red Army assistance), July 1973.
4. Athens airport massacre, August 1973.
5. Hijacking of KLM jet at Dubai.
6. Fuimicino Airport massacre.
7. Shell refinery incident in Singapore in collaboration with the Japanese Red Army, January 1974.
8. Hijacking of British jet to Amsterdam.
9. Seizure of OPEC office in Vienna in November 1975 in collaboration with "Carlos."
10. June 1976 hijacking of Air France jet airliner, Athens to Entebbe.
11. Armed assault on El Al passengers in Yesilkoy Airport, Istanbul.

The second terror organization of the Rejection Front is the Popular Front for the Liberation of Palestine—General Command (PFLP-GC) which is headed by Ahmad Jibril, also known as "Abu Jihad." It advocates a firm refusal to take part in a political solution to the Palestinian problem; denounces the PLO policy of a limited solution to the Palestinian territorial problem; and calls for the overthrow of rightist Arab governments. PFLP-GC terrorist operations since 1968 are the following:

1. Hijacking of an El Al airliner (a significant first in Palestine air hijack operations which ushered hijacking into the modus operandi of the Palestinian terrorists), 1968.
2. Attack on an El Al airliner in Zurich, 1969.
3. Hijacking of a TWA airliner, 1969.
4. June 1975 kidnap of a U.S. Army colonel in Beirut.

The PFLP-GC is not tightly organized or structured and is held together primarily by the leadership qualities of Jibril.

The Black June Organization (BJO) with its headquarters in Bagdad is led by Sabri al Banna, also known as "Abu Nidal." It is a pro-Iraqi organization named to protest the June 1976 Syrian intervention in the war in Lebanon. Its political orientation is to disrupt and destroy any effort toward a political reconciliation of the Mideast conflict as well as to overthrow the Saudi, Egyptian, and Kuwaiti regimes. The BJO's terrorist activities include the following:

1. The hijacking of a BOAC plane to Tunis, November 1974.
2. Seizure of a hotel and hostages in Damascus, September 1976.
3. The assault against Syrian Embassies in Rome and in Islamabad, October 1976.
4. The assault against the Intercontinental Hotel in Aman.

Other Palestinian terror organizations include the Front for the Liberation of Palestine (FLP), the Popular Democratic Front for the Liberation of Palestine (PDELP), the Arab Liberation Front (ALF), and the Popular Struggle Front (PSF). These groups have not yet committed significant acts of international terrorism. Their activities have centered on across-border operations into Israel. Broken down by organization these terror acts are as follows:

PDELP: May 1974, Schoolhouse massacre in Ma'alot, Israel. November 1974, attacked Bet Ahe'ansan settlement.

FLP: None known to date.

ALF: December 1974, bombings at Hanita, Israel. June 1975, kidnappings at Kfar Yuval Kibbutz.

PSF: May 1975, bombed the Israeli resort of Ein Fesh-'ha. June 1975, kidnap of a U.S. Army Colonel in Beirut (in collaboration with PFLP-GC).

Palestinian terror groups target their operations against buildings, installations, and airlines. Since they operate from a third country sanctuary, it is extremely difficult for them to make precise attack plans against persons. Almost without exception, the only time Palestinian terror group plan or participate in assassination operations are when such operations are in Arab countries where the terrorists can blend into the population. In all other cases, the acts of terrorism are committed to take hostages, which are then used as a means to escape back to their sanctuary.

Terror in Iran

Iran, of course, has supported terrorist movements for sometime. Yet it is difficult to point to one specific time in Iran and say it was here that terrorism began. Most observers might agree the catalyst was probably the Shah's reform program, which severely aggravated conservative Muslim religious leaders. In protest against modern reform, large scale religious riots flared up in Teheran. The government responded with military force and an estimated 700 people were killed in May, 1963. The Ayatollah Khomeini was arrested and exiled to Iraq, and the stage was set for terrorism.

The first Iranian terror group was the Mujahidin, or the People's Strugglers, an urban guerrilla organization composed mainly of middle class and university types. Shortly after its birth, the Mujahidin aligned itself closely with Palestinian terror groups. It not only trained in Palestinian camps, but also fought in Israel with Palestinian guerrillas. Because of this early training the Mujahidin, although operating within Iran as an internal terrorist group, adopted the modus operandi of the Palestinian terrorists. It soon became the military action spearhead of the conservative religious groups led by Khomeini. The result: a strange but deadly alliance, with the religious groups providing the Mujahidin with finances and manpower. The Mujahidin was also supported by the Iranian National Front and the Confederation of Iranian Students which, although outlawed in Iran, functioned in both Europe and the United States.

Ideologically, the Mujahidin, the National Front, the Confederation of Iranian Students, and the followers of Khomeini believed in a forced return to traditional Islamic religious values. Violently anti-American, they used terror as a tactic to win their political goals. The Mujahidin was totally terror-prone. They attacked with anything and everything, generally killing their victims with such a preponderance of force that it was like using a hammer to swat flies. On May 6, 1975 the Mujahidin shot down and killed one of their own group, Majid Sharif Vaghefi, fearing he was about to betray them. After killing him, his former comrades took his body into the country where they cut it open, filled the corpse with explosives, and set the body on fire. The exploded body was a warning to those who would betray the Mujahidin.

One of the Mujahidin's preferred targets was Americans, preferably easily identified uniformed Americans. Among the Mujahidin's victims:

1. U.S. Army colonel murdered in June, 1973.
2. Two U.S. Air Force officers killed in May, 1975.
3. Three U.S. civilians assassinated in August, 1976.

The Marxist ideology of the Mujahidin comes from three sources. The first is the Confederation of Iranian Students, who brought back Marxist and Maoist theories learned in European and U.S. universities in the 1960's. Another influx of Marxism occurred when the Mujahidin absorbed the remnants of the Siah Kal guerrillas, a Maoist rural guerrilla band decimated by the Iranian Army in the province of Gilan in 1971. The defeat of the Siah Kal spelled the end of rural guerrilla warfare in Iran and turned the terrorist focus to urban warfare.

The larger part of their communist ideology came through the operational liaison the Mujahidin effected with another, larger terror group, the Charikhaye Feda'i-yi Kalq or "Chariks," (People's Sacrifice Guerrillas). The Chariks are directly descended from the Tudeh, the Iranian Communist Party, in itself a terror group. In November, 1970, the Tudeh tried to kidnap American Ambassador Douglas MacArthur III but were thwarted by the Ambassador's alert chauffeur, who sped out of the trap. After joining the Mujahidin, the Chariks indoctrinated the Mujahidin leadership with Marxist philosophy. Communist doctrine permeated the ranks and was accepted by the religious majority, perhaps as an evil, but an evil necessary to win political goals. The Charik's modus operandi differed from the Mujahidin, as the Chariks preferred to kill Iranian officials rather than Americans. Nonetheless the Chariks and Mujahidin teamed together successfully in terror operations.

On December 30, 1974 a Charik hit team assassinated Ali Gholi Niktaba of the Iranian National Police. Two months later on March 3, 1975 a Mujahidin hit team killed Captain Yakullah Nowruzi, the chief of security of Aryamehr University. Both teams, one Mujahidin, the other Charik, were commanded by the Charik terrorist leader, Khashayyar Sanjari. While the Chariks and the Mujahidin were internal terrorists, operating and hiding in their own environment, their Palestinian modus operandi was as follows:

1. A comprehensive casing of the target was done before the execution of the act of terror by a team from the organization's support mechanism. The support team and the hit team are compartmented from each other in the same way as in the Popular Front for the Liberation of Palestine. On one occasion the tactic misfired. On July 3, 1975 a Mujahidin hit team killed one of their own members, mistaking him for a U.S. official. The hit team had no way of knowing this. The previous casings were done by the support team, and the hit team relied upon the information given to them that the American target would be inside the vehicle at the given time. Instead a Mujahidin member rode in the American's place.

2. The execution of the act of terror was done by the hit team made up of five members. Iranian female terrorists have often been the most militant. One, Samin Salehi, Iran's first female surgeon, was captured in September 1974 following a violent, bloody firefight on a crowded street.

3. Assassination victims in cars at the scene of the ambush were blocked-in by a terrorist vehicle.

4. Disguised in police and army uniforms, the terrorists reached point-blank range of the victim.

5. The terrorist hit teams used overwhelming firepower.

6. After shooting the victim the terrorists bombed or burned the victim's car and body.

7. If intercepted at any point by the police the terrorists resisted and attacked the police. If overcome, the terrorist committed suicide by swallowing poison capsules in order to avoid interrogation.

The modus operandi of the Mujahidin and the Chariks was a formidable one. The best defense for the intended victim was to vary his routes of travel, his time of travel, and be generally unpredictable. In every known case involving the Mujahidin and the Chariks, where the intended victim varied his time and route and acted unpredictably, the operation against him did not proceed to the execution stage. The Mujahidin and the Chariks feared the Iranian security forces and would not chance an operation against a security-minded target. Neither the Mujahidin nor the Chariks were invulnerable. An interesting case proving this point involved the Charik's leader, Hamid Ashraf, and the police work which led to his demise.

On several occasions the police raided Ashraf's headquarters or safehaven, but each time he escaped. The police then studied Ashraf's modus operandi, going back over each case. They found that each time they surrounded Ashraf, he sent his underlings out through the front door. Meanwhile, he took advantage of the firefight to escape over the roofs. During the next raid the police stationed a SWAT team on the rooftops. As predicted, Ashraf tried to escape over the roofs and was killed by the SWAT team's gunfire.

Iran's Collapse

In 1978, under Soviet direction, the Palestine Liberation Organization (PLO) and the Rejection Front began large scale training of People's Strugglers and the People's Sacrifice Guerrillas. Their goal was to overthrow the Shah of Iran and his pro-Western government. Their timing could not have been better. Iran was reeling from terrorist acts committed by the People's Strugglers and other terrorist groups. The military forces responded violently against the terrorists. Curfews, checkpoints, and martial law were put in effect. The Foco theory proved effective, and small groups of men and women had made a revolution where none had existed.

Beneath the surface Iran was seething with issues which the terrorist groups exploited. Similar to Latin America and other underdeveloped countries, Iran's birth rate was one of the highest in the world. A mammoth migration from the rural areas brought unskilled workers into the cities who could perform only manual labor. Thousands upon thousands of students from illiterate families were sent to universities and colleges in the United States and Europe where they succumbed to Marxist techniques. They were contacted by KGB officers who since 1974 had assigned Iranian students a high intelligence priority. Unfortunately, the majority of the Iranian students studied liberal arts instead of medicine, the sciences, and engineering. Those who returned to Iran joined the ranks of the unemployed and were further embittered by the many foreign technicians working in Iran at high salaries.

The PLO quickly went to work. It formed training cadres and began to train Iranians in urban guerrilla tactics. It also began to smuggle weapons and ammunition into Iran but soon recognized the enormity of the project. The PLO realized it could not complete the mission alone. The prize, Iran, was so rich it could be shared with others. Old differences were forgotten and compromises were made. The PLO and the Rejectionist Front, notably the Popular Front for the Liberation of Palestine (PFLP), joined forces and trained thousands of Iranian terrorists. Training camps were established in Lebanon, Syria, the People's Democratic Republic of Yemen (PDRY), Cyprus, Libya, and Iran itself. All other Palestinian terrorist activity was suspended in order to concentrate on Iran. 1978 was free of Palestinian terrorism because of their dedication to this new mission. Upwards of 5,000 Iranian terrorists were processed through the Palestinian training schools at a cost of about $30 million.

Members of the Japanese Red Army went to Cuba to expedite the training of PFLP terrorists. On graduation they were sent to train Iranians at the PFLP training school in Badar Garrison, People's Democratic Republic of Yemen. The Japanese Red Army did not engage in terrorist acts in 1978 but also dedicated itself to the Iranian mission. At the same time PLO members were sent to Pakistan to study advanced military subjects including fighter pilot training, naval courses, and armored tactics. A concerted effort was made to recruit military officers in other Arab countries. In India the representative of Ayatollah Khomeini told students at the University of Punjab that Khomeini and Yassar Arafat supported each other's causes and that the next Islamic movement would be that of the Palestinians. Palestinian terrorism was to become a *Jihad,* a holy war.

Palestinian cadres infiltrated into Iran and joined with the People's Strugglers and the People's Sacrifice Guerrillas to hasten the fall of the government. A spate of new, smaller terrorist organizations seemed to arise out of nowhere. The government of Iran collapsed, strangled by a crimson web of terror, before the Western world knew what had happened. Every status quo intelligence group had malfunctioned at the same time, and the massive Palestinian effort went undetected until their mission was accomplished.

Saudi Arabia

The next similar terrorist target is likely to be Saudi Arabia and the Persian Gulf area, the last source of Western oil in the Mideast. They are surrounded by terrorists. Saudi Arabia with all its wealth will be an easier target than Iran. The murder of one or two royal families may be enough to change the course of Saudi and world history. The fate of the Western world may be decided by a handful of bullets.

Philippine Terror Organizations

Asia's trouble spot is the Philippines, which has two terror organizations. The first is the Moro National Liberation Front (MNLF) and the second is the New People's Army (NPA).

The MNLF is located in the southern islands of the Philippines, principally Mindanao. It is a Muslim movement whose goal is political autonomy for the Muslim region. The MNFL engages in guerrilla warfare and is classified as an international terrorist organization because it kidnaps foreign officials and hijacks aircraft. A cease-fire signed in January 1977 between the Philippine government and the MNLF resulted in a temporary slowdown of activities, but random acts of terror continue.

The NPA is located in the mountains of the northern Philippines. It is a guerrilla army of the pro-Chinese Communist Party and is committed to rural revolution. Assassination is used as a terror tactic. In 1974 three U.S. Naval officers were killed near the navy base at Subic Bay.

The situation is presently in check and will remain so until there is a political change in the Philippine government. At that time the situation will probably worsen. At stake are the U.S. Naval base at Subic Bay, Clark Air Force Base, and three quarters of a century of Philippine/U.S. friendship.

Causes of European Terrorism

It is in Europe, however, that terrorism is in full swing. I have asked many Europeans why terrorism has taken hold in Europe. The answers are as follows:

1. There are numerous foreign laborers in Europe who support terrorist movements.
2. Foreign students are present in great numbers and organize and lead terrorist movements.
3. There are numerous political exiles in Europe who agitate and cause trouble.
4. There are many foreign terrorist targets in Europe.
5. There are few travel restrictions and an ease of movement across frontiers.
6. Many European countries have poor security practices.

The reasons may seem superficial. Something more is needed to account for the rise of terror in highly civilized countries.

Terrorism in Italy, where the political, economic, and social structures are in trouble, is easily understood. Some of Italy's biggest corporations are bankrupt. It is estimated that more than 50 billion dollars have been funneled out of the country. There are one million unemployed university graduates. Ten million non-Marxists voted for communist candidates. Two million people work in an inefficient civil service. In 1977, $36 million was paid out in ransom, making kidnapping Italy's most lucrative business.

Of the reported 115 terrorist groups in Italy, the best known is the Red Brigades. Its aim is to overthrow the Italian government and replace it with a communist regime. The Red Brigades grew from a communist political organization in Milan. In 1970 they adopted terrorism as a fundamental tactic. Their subsequent track record has been a bloody one of arson, kidnapping, robbery, sabotage, assassination, and the notorious "laming" of victims by shooting their kneecaps.

The rise of terrorism in Northern Europe, particularly Germany, is a strange development. The reasons why are not as clear as in Italy. A number of psychological reasons are given for its growth. One is that after World War II a number of governmental and civic institutions were formed in Germany to repress central authority and to decentralize the functions of government. Police functions were put at a state rather than a national level. During the German anti-Vietnam protests of the 1960's, strong political pressure at state levels limited police coverage of political and dissident German youth groups.

Another theory of terrorist causation is based upon the erosion of religious principles in Germany. This theory cites the fact that terrorism is a north German, not a south German, development. After World War II Northern Germany underwent a transformation from Calvinistic traditions to a center for prostitution and pornography. The young terrorists, with the zeal of Calvin's followers, attacked the establishments that permitted this moral deterioration.

Another theory is that with the end of the Vietnam war the many dissident groups in Germany disbanded. Only the diehards remained and became small terrorist groups. International relationships were facilitated by Wadi Haddad and his international training camps in Yemen, which gave European terrorists the opportunity to come together to train and exchange ideas. When they returned to their countries they took back with them what they had learned. Whatever the reason, terrorism in Germany is represented by the Baader-Meinhoff Gang, the Revolutionary Cells, and the 2 June Movement.

5

How Terrorists Operate

At 10 P.M., May 30, 1972, Air France flight 132 landed in Tel Aviv enroute from Paris and Rome. Three Japanese tourists disembarked and walked into the terminal where they retrieved their luggage. They opened their suitcases, took out automatic rifles and hand grenades, and began firing into the crowd.

The massacre continued until Yasuda Yasuyuki was killed. Ukudaira Takashi slipped on the bloody luggage conveyer belt and accidently exploded his own grenade, blowing off his head. Okamoto Kozo, the remaining terrorist, was tackled and captured while trying to escape.

Before Yasuda, Ukudaira, and Okamoto arrived at the Lod Airport, terrorist casing teams had done their work well. They observed the interior of the airport, the disposition of the airport security forces, and the location of passengers. Their report was then sent to terrorist headquarters. The completed plan was given to the Japanese Red Army hit team which practiced before carrying out their mission. The mission was to kill until they themselves were killed.

International Terrorist Operations

International and internal terrorists operate differently. An international terrorist group has greater limitations than an internal terrorist organization, because it is trying to focus on a target in another country, possibly thousands of miles away. It must send its members into another country, probably with false passports, to locate the victim and case the site selected for the attack. It cannot hover over its target as an internal group can. Because of this it uses different methods to deal with its victims.

The international terrorists organize themselves into three component parts. The first is the headquarters or the planning section, which is permanent. It decides what action shall be taken and how it should be done. To conduct an operation it recruits a support team and a hit team. Both are expendable and are recruited from one of the many Palestinian refugee camps prior to an action.

They always separate the casing team from the hit team, because the casing is done in a foreign country where the terrorists do not blend into the native population. The casing team is vulnerable, but if apprehended by the police, they are merely deported. However, if a team tried to do both the casing and the crime, it is likely to be caught with its weapons. Police treatment would then be far more harsh. The modus operandi now in use requires that one team only performs the casing. They then return home with their intelligence report. After weapons are sent into the country, the hit team follows and strikes the victim quickly before the local police uncover the plot.

Arms are smuggled across international borders in a number of ways. The arms used to hijack the Air France plane to Entebbe was concealed in a tin of olive oil. A simple method to pass weapons through airport X-ray devices is to disassemble a weapon and scatter the parts throughout the carry-on luggage. Inexperienced airport security personnel fail to discern that a weapon is being smuggled onboard. To pass through immigration controls, terrorists use false passports.

It is difficult for an international terrorist organization to plan road ambushes, kidnappings, bank robberies, and assaults from thousands of miles away. Instead they concentrate on fixed installations and specific, identifiable targets such as airlines. Their purpose is to take hostages to secure a means of escape to a country of refuge. For these reasons international terrorists attack embassies and international airline flights.

Japanese Red Army Operations

A typical example of the modus operandi used by an international terrorist organization is provided by the Japanese Red Army. The JRA has executed three hostage-taking operations in Asia and Europe: the attack on the Shell Refinery in Singapore in January 1974; the attack on the French Ambassador in the Hague in September 1974; and the seizure of the United States Embassy in Kuala Lumpur in August 1975. Study of these incidents reveals three JRA members are the organization's foremost leaders and hit men. They are Wako Harou, who took part in all three incidents, Yamada Yoshiaki, who participated in the Kuala Lumpur and Singapore attacks, and Ukudaira Junzo (the brother of Ukudaira Takashi who was killed in the Lod airport massacre), who participated in the Kuala Lumpur and Hague incidents. It must be remembered that Wako and Ukudaira conducted the Hague operation to obtain the release of Yakada, who was imprisoned in France.

The analysis of these incidents shows clearly that Wako, Ukudaira, Yamada, and the JRA use the same modus operandi as the Popular Front for the Liberation of Palestine (PFLP). In 1971 the pro-Soviet head of the PFLP aligned the JRA with the PFLP. The JRA moved its headquarters from Japan to the Beirut sanctuary of the PFLP and there learned and adopted the tactics of Wadi Haddad.

The JRA modus operandi can be summarized as follows:

1. Operating from a sanctuary, the JRA executes its acts of terror in other countries, always taking hostages as a means to provide their safe escape.

2. Because of their Japanese appearance, JRA members are not used for casing prior to the arrival of the hit team. They might attract attention and warn the victim. Instead, the JRA is always the hit team.

3. The JRA relies upon casing reports done by others. Sometimes the casings are good, other times faulty. While it was not a hostage-taking action, the preliminary casing which preceded the Lod Airport massacre was excellent; the Singapore Shell refinery casing, on the other hand was faulty. It would have resulted in a total failure had not a back-up PFLP operation in Aden relieved police pressure in Singapore.

4. The first minutes of a JRA hostage operation are prone toward violence. Within a few minutes, as the terrorists feel assured they have succeeded, they settle down and the level of terror used on the hostages subsides. The initial violence is not a part of JRA modus operandi but a Japanese characteristic of excitability in new situations. Once confi-

dence appears, the JRA terrorists become more reasonable in attitude and their treatment of hostages.

5. Despite a worldwide reputation of ferociousness, rightly deserved from the 26 deaths resulting from the Lod Airport massacre, the JRA has not yet killed in a hostage-taking incident.

6. The JRA is open to negotiations in hostage incidents. Thus far, the JRA has achieved its major goals. About a 20 percent negotiable factor can be obtained by police forces with the JRA attaining about 80 percent of what it started out to achieve. In this respect, the JRA is more flexible and easier to deal with than the Baader-Meinhoff Gang or the Red Brigades of Italy.

As a matter of interest, here are the last verified whereabouts of the 39 known JRA members:

1. North Korea	9
2. Beirut	13
3. Libya (now probably in Beirut)	4
4. Japan (returned through deportation)	9
5. Unknown	4

Internal Terrorist Operations

As mentioned, internal terrorists operate quite differently from international terrorists. Internal terrorists are not within a sanctuary but a hostile environment where they are constantly hunted by the local police. Their goal is to topple the government. Seldom do they become involved in a hostage-taking barricade operation because it is difficult to negotiate their way out. Instead internal terrorists strike quickly, commit the act of terrorism, and escape into the local environment. If a hostage is taken, the internal terrorist is inclined to kill him. If a live hostage is released, he is interrogated by the police and can furnish information and clues as to where he was detained and the identity of his abductors. In Germany, Spain, Italy, and Iran, hostages are killed, not released.

Internal terrorists use surveillance more so than international terrorists because internal terrorists blend into the environment, whereas international terrorists do not. The purpose of a terrorist surveillance is different from that of a police surveillance. A police surveillance aims at uncovering the suspect's contacts, while terrorists are not concerned with whom the victim sees. Their mission is to ascertain the victim's routine in order to select the best possible ambush site. With this difference in purpose there is a difference in modus operandi. Terrorists do not use a close-in police surveillance system, but instead hang back a block or two, in a car, motorcycle, or bicycle, impossible to detect.

Once the victim's routine is know, the ambush site is selected with three criteria in mind:

1. The location lends surprise to the attack.
2. The site is free of police.
3. Once or more escape routes are accessible.

The terrorists case the ambush site. They may visit the area for short periods or they may station one of their own there as a fixed surveillant for a long period of time. Disguises, such as repairmen or vendors, are frequently used. In the case of the assassination of the President of Spain, Carrero Blanco, the surveillant kept track of his routine for three months. A fixed surveillant is difficult to identify. He blends into the scene and has a simple, observation mission to fulfill:

1. Is the victim security conscious?
2. Are there police in the area at the time the victim passes through?
3. Is there any unusual activity in the area at the time the victim passes?

If the victim varies his routine, the terrorists have a difficult time selecting the ambush site and ascertaining whether it will be free of police when the ambush is to take place. He cannot be 100 percent certain of success.

When terrorists cannot select an ambush point on the victim's routine, either because none exists or because the victim varies his routine, the terrorists have the option of hitting the victim near his residence. This street, which the victim must transit because there is no other choice, is usually quiet and free of police. It is the only exit.

A number of interesting cases have taken place in close-in casings. There were four such recorded cases which involved Americans. One took place in Khartoum, the other three in Teheran. In Khartoum the American thought he was under a surveillance but told only his wife, and did nothing else. He was killed in a terrorist attack. In Teheran a pony-tailed woman in a European-style dress tried to gain entrance into the victim's homc. Shc was later seen loitering in the area on several occasions. The American did nothing. A few days later he was murdered, only a short distance from his home, by the People's Strugglers. Two other Americans in Teheran thought they were under surveillance and reported their suspicions to security officers. They were told to vary their routine and change their time of departure and arrival. They did so, and nothing happened to them nor did they notice any subsequent surveillance.

The Iranian police raided a number of safehouses used by the People's Strugglers and captured a large number of casing reports prepared by the terrorists. A study of these reports showed that when the intended victim displayed a sense of security, varied his route to work, and changed his time of departure and arrival, the terrorists dropped him as a target and chose another.

From internal terrorist case studies several important lessons have been learned:

1. The greatest deterrent to a terrorist attack is unpredictability of the victim. The variance of route or travel between the residence and the place of employment, and the changing of departure times is an excellent security precaution.

2. The victim should be alert to anything unusual happening in his neighborhood. Neighbors should be alerted to be on the lookout for suspicious actions. Native residents are more conscious of what is normal and what is not than short-term resident foreigners.

In addition to casing and surveillance, terrorists also penetrate offices, buildings, and factors to collect information which will help them seize the installation or its occupants. The penetration is done by a member of the terrorist organization who is employed in the installation, or more likely by a relative or friend of a terrorist who is coerced into the mission. The best defense against terrorist penetration of an installation is a continuing security investigation of all employees as well as discreet incentives to loyal employees to report suspicious and unusual happenings.

Balkan Terrorism

In contrast to the modus operandi of the Baader-Meinhoff Gang, the Red Brigades, and the Japanese Red Army, a different kind of terrorism originated in the Balkans. Based upon deeply felt social, political, and religious differences, the Croatian separatists, the Serbian monarchists, and the Yugoslav Internal Security Service (the Service for State Security) have waged a worldwide war of terror against each other for more than thirty years. The terror tactics used differ fundamentally in that the Croatian separatists are fringe groups or individuals of larger emigre communities, and the acts of terror are committed by individuals and not by organizations. For example, in an organization such as the Popular Front for the Liberation of Palestine it is the organization itself which plans, approves and executes the operation. With Croatian separatists the operation is totally conceived, planned, and executed by a few Croatian emigres. The operations are aimed at the enemy and not the public at large, as is the case with the Palestinian terrorists. Croatian separatists attack Yugoslav officials and installations. Serbians similarly attack Yugoslav officials and their installations. The Service for State Security kills both Croatian and Serbian emigre leaders.

Because these acts of terror are planned by individuals and not an organization, the operations are conducted at random. Targetting is precise but occasionally innocent bystanders are killed. In addition, on two occasions the Croatian separatists hijacked airliners and are now classified as international terrorists. The modus operandi is almost exclusively assassination by gun or bomb, and the methodology is blunt, almost military—a direct attack with little or no casing for surveillance. Blunt confrontation is difficult to defend against. Personal security, residential and installation security, armor, and guards are recommended.

By no means complete, the following is chronology of known acts of terror executed by Croatian separatists, Serbian monarchists and the Service for State Security:

1. February 18, 1968: A bomb exploded in the basement of the residence of the Yugoslavic ambassador to France. One killed, fourteen injured.
2. October 26, 1968: Three prominent anti-communist

Croatian emigre leaders were found murdered in a Munich apartment.

3. June 9, 1969: A bomb exploded in the Yugoslav consulate in Sidney.

4. June 30, 1969: The head of the Yugoslav mission in West Berlin was seriously wounded in an assassination attempt against him.

5. November 29, 1969: Yugoslav embassy in Canberra bombed.

6. February 10, 1971: Two Croatians seized control of the Yugoslav consulate in Goteborg.

7. April 7, 1971: Yugoslav ambassador to Sweden was killed and two Yugoslav diplomats wounded by Croatian separatists.

8. September 15, 1972: Three Croatian emigres hijacked a SAS airliner and ransomed its passengers for six Croatians held in Swedish jails. Sweden complied with ransom request. The terrorists found sanctuary in Paraguay. Later, on June 7, 1976 one of the same terrorists shot and killed the Uruguayan ambassador to Paraguay thinking that he was shooting the Yugoslav ambassador.

9. January 27, 1972: Bomb exploded on train enroute from Vienna to Zagreb and injured six people.

10. January 26, 1972: Yugoslav airliner enroute Stockholm to Begrade bombed. 26 killed.

11. June 20, 1972: 19 Croatian terrorists infiltrated Western Bosnia-Hercegovina and killed 13 local security officers before they were overcome.

12. September 17, 1972: Office of Yugoslav tourist agency in Sidney bombed.

13. December 8, 1972: American businessman killed in bomb blast emanating from vehicle parked outside Serbian church in Brisbane.

14. August 14, 1973: Belgrade railroad station bombed. One killed and seven injured.

15. March 30, 1975: Yugoslav vice-consul in Lyon shot and severely wounded.

16. June 23, 1975: Yugoslav mission to the United Nations bombed.
17. December 29, 1975: Home of Yugoslav consul in Chicago bombed.
18. January 3, 1976: Home of Yugoslav consul in Stuttgart bombed.
19. February 7, 1976: Yugoslav vice consul in Frankfurt assassinated.
20. June 28, 1976: Assassination attempt against Yugoslav vice consul in Dusseldorf.
21. August, 1976: Two Serbian monarchists murdered in Paris.
22. August 28, 1976: Croatian separatist killed in Nice, France when bomb inside his car exploded.
23. September 10, 1976: Four Croatians and one American hijacked a TWA airliner enroute from New York to Chicago.
24. November 28, 1977: Bomb discovered at Yugoslav consulate in Lyon.
25. December 3, 1977: Bomb exploded in Yugoslav airline office in Melbourne.
26. December 4, 1977: Bomb exploded in Hamburg-Belgrade train. No casualties.

Croatian terror continues to fester with some observers who believe that any change in the political status quo in Yugoslavia will trigger an explosion of terror, perhaps even civil war. Because of this potential, Croatian communities are watched closely by the Service for State Security and the Soviet KGB.

Little is known about the Armenian Secret Army for the Liberation of Armenia. But from its random acts of terror directed against the Turkish government, it appears similar in organization and modus operandi to the Croatian separatists. Both seek the liberation of a homeland. The history of Armenian terror is as follows:

1. January 27, 1973: The Turkish Consul General and the Vice Consul in Los Angeles were lured to Santa Barbara by Gourgen Yanikian on the pretext of business and were murdered. A psychiatric examination indicated Yanikian was insane.

2. April 4, 1973: The Turkish Consulate General and the Turkish airline office, both in Paris, were attacked.

3. February 20, 1975: The Beirut office of the Turkish airlines bombed. The Gourgen Yanikian group claimed responsibility.

4. October 22, 1975: The Turkish Ambassador in Vienna shot to death.

5. October 24, 1975: The Turkish Ambassador in Paris and his chauffeur murdered.

6. December 28, 1975: Rocket attack against the Turkish embassy in Beirut.

7. February 16, 1976: First Secretary of the Turkish embassy in Beirut assassinated.

8. June 2, 1978: The wife of the Turkish ambassador to Spain, his brother, and a Spanish chauffeur were murdered in Madrid.

Basque Terrorism

The Basque terrorist organization, the Euzkadi Ta Azkatuna (ETA, Basque Homeland and Freedom) is a homeland liberation movement with its support centered in the Basque speaking provinces of Alava, Vizcaya, and Guipuzcoa. Its victims are Spanish government officials.

The Basque struggle against the Spanish government dates back to the middle ages when the Basque nations were annexed to the Spanish kingdom. Briefly, during the period of the Spanish Civil War, the Spanish government in Madrid granted the Basques autonomy in return for their military support against the armies of General Franco, but with Franco's victory the autonomy was rescinded. The brief period of self-government added fuel to the fire of nationalism, but opposition was passive. It was not until the mid-1960s that the ETA was organized under the leadership of Julian de Madariaga and the aegis of Cuba. The ETA was born with ties by language to Cuba and by location to nearby Algeria.

Tactics of the ETA are basically the same as those of other internal terrorist organizations. A swift lightning attack is followed by a speedy retreat from the scene of action before the police arrive. Planning is a necessity. The tactic of murder is preferred, rather than the more dangerous hostage-taking techniques of international terrorists.

The ETA tactic of murder is based upon either assassination from a fixed point of ambush or by a moving ambush party. In one case which took place on October 4, 1976 Juan Maria de Araluce, a liberal member of the advisory Counselors of the Realm, was enroute home for lunch. His chauffeur-driven car was about to turn into the driveway of his home in San Sebastian when a concentrated hail of machinegun bullets raked the car and the trailing vehicle of police bodyguards. Mr. Araluce and three police bodyguards were killed. Five assassins sprang from their hidden ambush site and ran around the corner where their getaway car was parked, and escaped.

The tactic was a simple one: kill the victim suddenly and without warning by an overwhelming amount of firepower. It was identical to the method used by the People's Strugglers in Iran. The essential element is that the terrorists must know the victim's routine.

In another case, Augusto Uceta Barrenchea, the Basque President of the Provincial Council of Vizcaya, was driving to the gymnasium to play jai alai when his car was overtaken by another. As the passing car drew alongside, terrorists leaned through the windows and sprayed Uceta's car with machinegun fire, killing him. The terrorists sped away and escaped. The tactic of the moving ambush party was identical to the modus operandi used by the 2 June Movement in assassinating West German Prosecutor Siegfried Buback in Karsruhe. The essential information needed in this kind of murder is again the victim's precise routine.

The ETA is an internal terrorist group but it has the added capability of being able to operate from France into Spain. The ETA can kidnap and hold a hostage captive in France while it negotiates the hostage's release in Spain. If the ransom is paid, the ETA can release the hostage knowing there is little the hostage can tell the police which would lead to the arrest of his abductors.

The ETA has been able to continue operating in the French sanctuary by confining its terrorism to the Spanish Basque provinces. The two Basque provinces in France are free from terrorist attack. In turn, the French government does little to molest the ETA so long as the ETA maintains its low, non-violent profile on the French side of the frontier.

Because of the low risk modus operandi of the ETA and the luxury of its nearby sanctuary, it is a difficult organization to bring under control. Additionally, the ETA is able to exploit a long history of nationalist opposition to the Spanish government. It is able to count upon a political support base—something which the Baader-Meinhoff gang and other internal, anti-establishment terrorist organizations could not do. While only a small percentage of the Basque people condone the terror of the ETA, few are willing to help the Spanish government. Successes by the Spanish police are used by the ETA propagandists as further fuel against Spanish rule. For instance, Angel Otaequi, and ETA terrorist, was executed by a firing squad for killing a Spanish policeman. His body was taken to his native village of Nuarbe in the Basque region where it was buried. The Basque national flag of red, white, and green adorned the grave with the tombstone enscribed "Angel you have not died in vain."

Support for the ETA by the Basque people was expressed by a Basque priest on the eve of Basque worker strikes in 1976 when he said, "The whole world has become aware of the Basque problem because of the them (ETA)."

With this declaration, 1,500 Basque priests signed a document urging support for a worker's strike. Such support of a pro-Marxist terrorist organization by large numbers of Catholic priests is one of the rare characteristics of the ETA's potential. At least 50 percent of the Basque Catholic priests are ETA supporters. Passive support alone by so large a church body is of formidable assistance, but through passive support for the ETA, a number of Catholic priests have also become active militants. Eustaqui Mendizabal, a former Benedictine monk, became a leader of the ETA-military wing and was captured and executed in 1973. Reverend Juan Bautista, a Capuchin monk, was sentenced on June 7, 1975 to twelve years imprisonment for terrorist activities, specifically the illegal possession of explosives. Another example is Reverend Yon Etzabe Garitacelaya, now serving a fifty year prison sentence for terrorist activities. The Basque priests believe that they rarely rise in the Spanish church hierarchy and are therefore at odds with Spanish bishops who support the government.

History of the ETA

The ETA began in the mid-1960s during the political radicalization of Basque youth. It was the time of the rebellions in Algeria and Cuba. Both helped shape the future of the clandestine struggle in Spain. The political orientation and goals of the ETA were set at periodic meetings of respective ETA representatives in an ETA gathering known as an "assembly." The ETA-Fifth Assembly decided that their primary action against the Spanish government would be armed violence—a war of terrorism. Three years later the ETA-Sixth Assembly was held and a major dispute took place which split the ETA into two groups. One was the ETA-VI which adhered to conventional communist doctrines, both orthodox and Trotskyite. The other was the ETA-V which remained loyal to the armed action concepts agreed upon in the ETA-V Assembly.

The ETA-VI soon disappeared as an entity when it broke in two. One part fused with Liga Komunista Iraultzaile (LKI, Iraultzaile Communist League) while the other part became the Liga Communista Revolucionaria (LCR, Revolutionary Communist League). The LCR was Trotskyite in orientation and quickly established contact with the headquarters of the Fourth International. By this action the LCR became the third Trotskyite organization in Spain. The other two are the Partido Obrero Revolucionaria de Espana (PORS, Workers Revolutionary Party of Spain) and the Liga Komunista (LK, Communist League).

The Fourth International (FI) is a Trotskyite movement headquarterd in Brussels, Belgium. It takes its name from the fourth international meeting of communist world leaders. At that meeting the principles of Trotsky (as opposed to Stalin) were accepted. So instead of building socialism in one country first, it was agreed that the Soviet Union could be a springboard for worldwide revolution through the organization of workers.

Trotskyites still believe in these principles: (1) Worldwide revolution; and (2) Revolution through the organization of workers. Because of this, the Fourth International is at odds with Fidel Castro and the Foco theory because the Foco theory is totally unrelated to the workers' movement. A recent example of this conflict occurred in July 1979 when the triumphant FSLN expelled the Simon Bolivar

Brigade from Nicaragua to Colombia, solely because the brigade was Trotskyite and affiliated with Fourth International.

The ETA-V also split into two factions. The first became ETA-Military and the other ETA-Political Military. The ETA-Political Military believed political action was needed in addition to the use of terrorism. The ETA-Military, however, continued armed action and terrorism.

The ETA-Political Military soon broke into three parts. The majority formed the Party of the Basque Revolution (EIA). Little has been heard from this group. Another group splintered off to become the Berezis Commandos under the command of Miguel Angel Apalatequi. The remainder of the ETA-Political Military renounced armed struggled and proclaimed that henceforth it would concentrate on mass action.

Again the ETA-Military continued its course of armed action and terrorism without deviation and permitted the Brezis Commandos splinter group to fuse within the ETA-Military. The ETA-Military announced its missions and its goals:

1. To divide the Basque political parties and make the ETA-Military the dominant force within the Basque political picture.
2. To undermine the moderate political leaders who negotiate and compromise with the Spanish government to arrive at a peaceful settlement of the Basque issue.
3. To polarize the population to take sides—or as Marighella stated, "the population must either be on the side of the terrorist or if not, then too terrorized to take the side of the other."
4. To force the government through terrorists acts to implement repressive counterterrorist measures.

Since 1970 the ETA-Military has adhered to the Cuban Foco theory that a revolution can be made where none existed before.

The two communist parties, both the one sympathetic with Moscow and the other comprised of Trotskyites, oppose the ETA-Military. Their precepts reject the Foco theory and the principle that revolution can make a revolution. They charged that the armed action policy of the ETA-Military was a negative factor, and that the use of armed action was only a desperate attempt to substitute terror for mass action by the people. The ETA-Military continued to insist that revolution is made from the top down and not by organizing from the bottom up.

The communists also charged that ETA-Military leaders were not capable of grasping the evolution of the class struggle, and changing the ETA-Military's political activity to meet a new situation in Spain. The problem, the communists claim, is bigger than destroying the government in the Basque region; the problem is one of toppling the Spanish government in all of Spain.

In summation, the communists state, "If the ETA-Military continued its present political line, it will end its political career as an organization far removed from the realities of the class struggle, insensitive to political changes, peripheral to the workers and mass movements, and rejected by its own people."

In answer the ETA-Military stepped up its program of terror in 1978:

1. January 11, 1978: Policeman killed.
2. February 14, 1978: Policeman killed.
3. March 5, 1978: Three policemen killed, two wounded.
4. March 16, 1978: One policeman killed, one wounded.
5. March 22, 1978: Government official killed.
6. May 9, 1978: Policemen attacked, two killed and four wounded.
7. June 21, 1978: Policeman killed.
8. June 26, 1978: Army general killed.
9. August 29, 1978: Four policemen killed.
10. October 3, 1978: Naval officer killed.
11. October 9, 1978: Two policemen killed.
12. November 5, 1978: Policeman killed.

The ETA-Military also maintains and consolidates its contacts with other terrorist groups. By the end of 1978 it had contacts with the Cubans, the Irish Republican Army, the Brittany Separatist Front, the Polisario in Algeria, the Algerians, and others, with frequent reports of ETA-Military training in Algeria and Cuba.

6

Terrorist Connections

Counterterrorists have looked for connections between terrorist organizations but have not been as successful as they wished. The reason is that police tactics were used and clues were sought in the same manner as in criminal cases. However, the terrorist problem is political, not criminal, and many of the clues were not hidden, but out in the open, published in the press. Terrorist organizations are not separate, isolated groups but are more of an international political movement. Terrorists know each other. They loan money, documents, and weapons to each other. They take part in each other's operation and lend a helping hand whenever they can. Nowhere is this more true than in Europe.

In a historical perspective, the fire for modern European terrorism came from European intellectual circles in the mid-1950's. It quickly spread to universities, magazines, fashionable circles, and finally permeated the upper middle class. It was fashionably elite to be of the radical left, the "chic left." In affluent Western Germany, it was said that so much was given to the children of WW II that little was left to give, except the moral superiority of radical leftist politics and the free sex of commune living.

Origins of German Terrorism

It is impossible, of course, to summarize the development of German terror in a few paragraphs, but there would be little disagreement among counterterrorists to list the cornerstone of German terror as:

1. The pro-communist magazine *Konkret,* published by Klaus Rainer Rohl, the husband of terrorist Ulrike Meinhoff.

2. The Free University of Berlin.

3. Siegfried Haag, the German lawyer and founder of the Socialist Lawyers Collective.

4. Horst Mahler, a radical lawyer and mentor to the Baader-Meinhoff gang and the Red Army Faction.

5. Andreas Baader, the militant who led the transformation from passive opposition to terror.

6. Gudrun Ennslin, who gave communist political substance to Baader's militancy.

7. Ulrike Meinhoff, who tried to imbue Baader's terrorism with political immortality.

The followers, the young, unhappy Germans, became rank and file terrorists who killed and burned and either died or went to jail. There is no question; they were *used.* They were used by publications such as *Konkret.* They were used by the university professors. They were used by people such as Rohl, Mahler, and Haag. They were used by the communist movement.

In the beginning the anti-establishment, anti-American protest was considered a student movement, but in the late 1960s changed to terror. The movement ran out of causes and began to wane, and the protest movement began to disband. After his arrest in 1978 Horst Mahler explained, "After 1968 and 1969 we saw the wave of the movement was dying. They were two opposing ideas about what to do: Join ongoing struggles in factories, neighborhoods and universities; or develop an abstract guerrilla warfare as part of the third world revolution. The Red Army Faction chose the latter. I was trapped."

As Mahler said, international terrorism broke out in Germany in the latter 1960s. Shortly before it did, an interesting event took place. Andreas Baader and Gudrun Ensslin fled Germany in the summer of 1968 to escape sentencing for a series of Frankfurt department store fires they had set. Joined by Ingrid Proll, the trio went to Paris, where they lodged in the apartment of Regis DeBray. At that time Debray was imprisoned in Bolivia for collaboration in revolutionary activities with Che Guevara while helping to prepare Guevara's book on the Cuban theories of revolution and guerrilla warfare, *Revolution Within A Revolution.* The German trio then traveled to Colombia, where Baader was briefly jailed, and after his release went to Italy, Switzerland, and West Berlin. In Berlin the trio was welcomed back by Mahler and a newcomer to the underground, Ulrike Meinhoff. Their war of terror was about to begin.

The Baader-Meinhoff Gang

From the standpoint of counterterrorism the trip by Baader and his companions must be equated to some revolutionary purpose which required financing by other persons. Contact was probably established with other revolutionary groups such as the Colombian Revolutionary Armed Forces (FARC), the Petra Krause organization in Switzerland, and the forerunners of the Red Brigades in Italy—all places where Baader had traveled.

The following is the chronology of terror of the Baader-Meinhoff gang/Red Army Faction:

1. May 11, 1972: A bomb exploded in the U.S. Army Officer's Club in Frankfurt. One killed, thirteen injured. Subsequently Dierk Hoff was arrested as the bomb-maker of the Baader-Meinhoff gang.

2. May 24, 1972: Two bombs exploded in U.S. Army Headquarters in Heidelberg. One killed, two wounded.

3. June 10, 1972: The West German Embassy in Dublin was bombed by supporters of the Baader-Meinhoff Gang, possibly the Irish Republican Army.

4. January 13, 1975: Johannes Weinrich, using documentation stolen by the Baader-Meinhoff Gang in the alias of Klaus Mueller, took part in a Palestinian terrorist attack on an Israeli airliner at the Orly airfield in Paris.

5. April 24, 1975: Six West German terrorists, members of a Baader-Meinhoff hit team called the "Holger Meins Commandos," seized the West Germany Embassy in Stockholm. (As a part of the modus operandi, West German hit teams are named after terrorist who were killed or died.) Holger Meins was a Baader-Meinhoff member who was arrested with Baader and Jan Carl Raspe on June 1, 1971. His arrest was televised and he was clad only in shorts to show he was unarmed. Meins let off a series of unearthly screams as he was dragged off by the police. *The Eight Howls of Holger Meins* was a television hit. He died in prison on November 9, 1974 because of his self-imposed

hunger strike. The following day the 2 June Movement assassinated Judge von Drenkman in Berlin.

The members of the "Holger Meins Commandos" were:

A) Hanna-Elise Krabbe born 1954, a member of the Socialist Patient's Collective (SPK) of Heidelberg and part of the Baader-Meinhoff gang. Dr. Wolfgang Huber organized the Socialist Patient's Collective. It derived its name from the belief by its members that society was sick.
B) Lutz Manfried Taufer, born March 1944, a SPK member.
C) Karl Heina Dellwo, born 1952, a SPK member.
D) Bernard Maria Roessner, born 1946, probably affiliated with SPK.
E) Siegfried Hausner, born 1952, a SPK explosive expert who died in a German prison as a result of wounds sustained in an explosion in the Stockholm seizure.

In making the Stockholm assault, the six terrorists rushed into the W. German Embassy, firing their automatic weapons in the air. They seized the ambassador and eleven other members of the embassy as hostages and killed the military attache. The objective of the attack was to obtain the release of Andreas Baader, Ulrike Meinhoff, and twenty-four other terrorists. When the terrorists were told that the West German government refused to meet the ransom demands, the terrorists shot and killed another hostage, the economic attache. They then set off explosive charges as retreat cover, but were apprehended by the Swedish police and returned to Germany.

6. May 3, 1975: Two bombs exploded at the construction site of a French nuclear power station at Fessenheim near the West German border. Responsibility for the attack was claimed by the "Puig-Antich Ulrike Meinhoff Commando," an obvious tie-in between the Baader-Meinhoff gang and Spanish counterparts.

Salvador Puig Antich, a Spanish terrorist, was executed in Spain on March 2, 1974 for killing a police officer. He was executed by garroting because the military authorities refused him the honor of a firing squad. The garrot is a Spanish death device which dates back to 1400 A.D. It consists of an iron neck collar tightened by a long screw which the executioner turns until the bound victim either dies of strangulation or a broken neck.

7. The "Puig Antich-Ulrike Meinhoff Commandos" bombed the West German consulate in Nice, France.

8. July 4, 1976: Two Baader-Meinhoff terrorists, Wilfried Boese and Brigitte Kuhlmann, who joined with Palestinian terrorists to hijack an Air France airliner, were killed by Israeli rescue forces at Entebbe.

9. July 30, 1977: Suzanne Albrecht, a one-time employee of lawyer Klaus Croissant, escorted her friends into the Frankfurt home of Juergen Ponto, her family's longtime friend. Ponto was head of the Dreshner Bank, one of West Germany's big three clearing banks. When he resisted kidnapping he was fatally shot. A dragnet went out for Albrecht as well as other young, former employees of Croissant. The list included Elizabeth von Dyck, who helped Siegfried Haag purchase weapons in Switzerland; Silke Maier-Witt who became a suspect in the murder of Hans-Martin Schleyer; Angelika Speitel, a suspect in the murder of Siegfried Buback and Willy Peter Stoll, also a Schleyer murder suspect. Speitel's husband also worked for Croissant. The web which Croissant had spun was nebulous and included young terrorists from various organizations such as the Baader-Meinhoff Gang as well as the 2 June Movement. Hans-Joachim Klein, a leading member of the 2 June Movement, was a driver and messenger for Croissant. When Berlin lawyer Horst Mahler arranged the visit of Jean-Paul Sartre to Baader's prison cell, Klein was the driver. The network was interlocking.

10. September 5, 1977: During the evening rush hours, the three car convoy of Hans-Martin Schleyer sped through Cologne. Schleyer was West Germany's foremost industrialist and president of the Federal Union of German Industry. A baby carriage was pushed into the street in front

of the convoy. The cars braked to a stop. A van pulled alongside and five terrorists, four men and a woman, strafed the convoy with automatic weapons. Two policemen and a guard were killed; Schleyer became a kidnap victim.

The Schleyer Manhunt

In return for Schleyer the terrorists demanded the release of eleven terrorists in prison. The list included Andreas Baader, Gudrun Ensslin, Jan Carl Raspe, and those who took part in the assault on the West German Embassy in Stockholm. Negotiations dragged on, and on October 19, 1977, the day after the rescue of the hijacked Air France hostages in Mogadiscio by the German GSG-9 team, the body of Schleyer was found in the trunk of an abandoned car in Mulhouse, France. Even before his abduction the German police thought that Schleyer was a terrorist target. They had reached this conclusion on the basis of papers and plans found in the office of lawyer Siegfried Haag after his arrest. Schleyer had been warned.

The police investigation of the Schleyer murder identified the prime suspects as Frederike Krabbe, Christoph Wackernagel, Rolf Heissler, Stefan Wisniewski, Willy Peter Stoll, and Monika Helbing.

A painstakingly slow but relentless manhunt began. As a result of wanted posters distributed by the West German police throughout Europe, the Dutch police spotted Wackernagel in Amsterdam on November 11, 1977. Wackernagel and his companion resisted arrest and opened fire on the police. In the gunfight both Wackernagel and his companion, Gert Richard Schneider, were severely wounded. Wackernagel was a student of cinema photography and during Schleyer's captivity, Wackernagel took movie and video photographs of Schleyer's ordeal.

On May 11, 1978 the French police arrested Stefan Wisniewski in the Paris airport and deported him to Germany. Wisniewski was found to be a courier between German terrorist groups and the Near East. In the summer of 1976 he received terrorist training in the People's Democratic Republic of Yemen. Also trained there were Siegfried Haag, Gabriele Krocher-Tiedemann, Verna Becker, and Fredericke Krabbe, the sister of Hanna Krabbe, who participated in the Stockholm attack on the West German Embassy.

Handwriting experts confirmed that Willy Peter Stoll wrote the rental check for the apartment in which Schleyer was confined. Fingerprints showed that Monika Helbing had occupied the apartment.

Willy Peter Stoll was killed by the police in Dusseldorf on September 6, 1978 while resisting arrest.

The day after Wackernagel and Schneider were shot and apprehended in Amsterdam, Ingrid Schubert heard the news in her cell in Stuttgart's Stammheim prison. Using the sheets off her cot as a rope, she hanged herself.

Rolf Heissler was arrested by Germany police on June 9, 1979 in Karlsruhe.

On November 19, 1979 the Swiss police arrested Rolf Wagner, a long-sought Baader Meinhoff member, for participation in the kidnap-murder of Schleyer. Wagner was arrested after a shoot-out in an underground shopping center in Zurich's banking and business center. The police said that three other gunmen escaped after the gunbattle during which a woman bystander was killed and three people wounded.

Elizabeth Von Dyck, who was sought by the West German authorities for her participation in the kidnap-slaying of Hans-Martin Schleyer, was fatally wounded on May 4, 1979 in a shootout with police in a terrorist hideaway near Nuremberg. When the police tried to arrest her she pulled out a large caliber pistol and the police opened fire.

The modus operandi of the Schleyer case is sometimes compared with the abduction of Aldo Moro in Rome to show a connection between the Baader-Meinhoff Gang and the Red Brigades. Both involved the ambush of a moving vehicle. In one case the victim's car was brought to a halt by a blocking vehicle. In the other a baby carriage was shoved in front of the approaching vehicle. In both cases the bodyguard was killed by concentrated, overwhelming firepower. Here the similiarity ends, except in both cases the victim was killed.

The Schleyer case was the beginning of the end for the Baader-Meinhoff Gang. The German people were repulsed by Schleyer's murder. People such as waiters and innkeepers began to inform on the whereabouts of terrorists. The police stepped up their counterterrorist operation. The communist parties and the radical left felt themselves threatened by terrorist attacks and even they withdrew their support. Finally, the Baader-Meinhoff Gang began to crack apart internally.

An overall analysis of Baader-Meinhoff operations reveals that the modus operandi of these German terrorists lacked sophistication. Instead, it developed along the lines of a *blitzkrieg*: lightning attacks accompanied by heavy firepower. Only in a few cases, such as in the Schleyer ambush, is there a glimpse of prior planning and casing. In the balance it was difficult for the Baader-Meinhoff Gang to do either extensive planning or casing. They were for the most part underground. Their photographs and descriptions were posted everywhere, and even cursory casings of an action site could be dangerous for them. The lesson learned is that when police pressure is applied and the terrorists are on the run, they cannot plan their operations well and are likely to make mistakes.

The 2 June Movement

Another terrorist organization active in Germany during the time of the Baader-Meinhoff Gang was the 2 June Movement, named after an incident which occured on June 2, 1967 in Berlin when a policeman shot and killed Benno Obnesorg, a student, during an anti-Shah demonstration. Unlike the Baader-Meinhoff Gang, whose members came from the upper middle class, the 2 June Movement was of a lower class origin. The Baader-Meinhoff Gang spent considerable time and effort in theoretical and academic discussion of communism and class struggle. The unregimented 2 June Movement, however, acted bluntly and directly in their application of terror.

The following is a chronology of the terrorist acts committed by the 2 June Movement:

1. February 2, 1972: The British Yacht Club in Berlin was bombed.
2. May 4, 1972: Turkish Consulate in Berlin bombed.
3. January 29, 1974: Gas lines at 22 Berlin gasoline stations severed.
4. November 10, 1974: On the day after Holger Meins died as a result of a prison hunger strike, three members of the 2 June Movement entered the home of Judge von Drenkmann in Berlin. As a pretext they passed themselves

off as florist's delivery men. When von Drenkmann resisted their kidnap attempt, he was shot and killed. The police identified his murderers as Ralf Reinders, the head of the 2 June Movement, and Andreas Vogel. Reinders was arrested on September 9, 1975; also arrested with him were Inge Viett and Julian Plambecke, both members of the 2 June Movement.

5. February 27, 1975: The Chairman of the Berlin Christian Democratic Union, Peter Lorenz, was kidnapped by the 2 June Movement and the ransom demanded was the release of German terrorists in prison. Significantly, the release of Andreas Baader and Ulrike Meinhoff was not requested. The West German government complied with the ransom request.

As a result, the following 2 June Movement terrorists were released from prison and flown to the People's Democratic Republic of Yemen where they obtained terrorist training:

1. Verena Becker, born 1952, returned to Germany and was later implicated in the murder of Siegfried Buback. Along with Guenter Sonnenberg, she resisted police arrest in Singen, Germany and was wounded and arrested. On April 26, 1978 she was sentenced to life imprisonment.

2. Ingrid Siepmann, born 1944, stayed on with the Palestinians for at least a year working in a medical center. Subsequently Siepmann was implicated in the Ponto murder in Frankfurt and the Palmer kidnap in Vienna.

3. Gabriele Kroecher-Tiedemann, born 1951, returned to German terror circles and assisted "Carlos" and Hans-Joachim Klein in the seizure of the OPEC offices in Vienna. Later she became involved in the kidnapping of Viennese businessman Walter Michael Palmers, and was arrested in Delemont, Switzerland on December 20, 1977 along with Christian Moeller. They were found to be in possession of ransom money paid for Palmer's release. While Kroecher-Tiedemann was a 2 June Movement member, Moeller was a member of the Communist Party of Germany and of the Red Help organization. On December

20, 1977 a Swiss court sentenced Kroecher-Tiedemann to 15 years in prison and Moeller to 11 years.

4. Rolf Rohl, born 1942, was rearrested in Greece on July 21, 1976 and returned to Germany.

The German police implicated the following 2 June Movement members in the Lorenz kidnapping:

1. Ralf Reinders, in prison.
2. Henrick Reinders.
3. Paul Reverman.
4. Angela Luther.
5. Werner Sauber, born the son of a Swiss millionaire. Sauber was killed in a police crossfire in Cologne on May 10, 1975 in a police shootout. Sauber did underground contact missions between the German Communist Party and the 2 June Movement.
6. Andreas Vogel, arrested in Berlin on March 26, 1976 and imprisoned with Ralf Reinders.
7. Eberhard Dreher was sentenced on March 23, 1978 to four years imprisonment for complicity in the Lorenz kidnapping.
8. Fritz Tuefel was arrested September 1975 and is imprisoned in Germany.

An unusual operation ended on March 30, 1977 when the Swedish police broke up a plot to kidnap a Swedish government minister. In cracking down on the terrorists the police discovered a large arsenal of assorted weaponry. The foreigners involved in the plot were expelled from Sweden. They were:

1. Norbert Eric Kroecher, German, the husband of Gabriele Kroecher-Tiedemann.
2. Manfred Richard Adomeit, German.
3. Alan Hunter, English.
4. Armando Gonzalez Carrillo, Mexican.
5. Tomas Okusuho Martinez, Mexican. Both Okusuho and Gonzalez Carrillo had hijacked a plane from Mexico to Cuba and later gained entry from Cuba to Sweden.
6. Maria Christina Fuetes, Chilean. She later married Gonzalez Carrillo.
7. Anna Maroufidou, Greek.

The modus operandi planned for the kidnapping was judged to be identical to the Lorenz kidnapping in Berlin. This was logical since the 2 June Movement was the terrorist organization for both incidents.

April 7, 1977: Federal Prosecutor Siegfried Buback and his chauffeur were gunned down in Karlsruhe. A manhunt began for the following 2 June Movement members:

1. Guenter Sonnenberg. On April 26, 1978 Sonnenberg was sentenced to life imprisonment after his capture following a police shootout in Singen, Germany. Reportedly he is under psychiatric care which is believed will be of lifetime duration.

2. Verena Becker, captured with Sonnenberg in the May 3, 1977 shootout in Singen, Germany and sentenced to life imprisonment.

3. Knut Folkers, captured in Utrecht, Netherlands following a police shootout in December 1977 and sentenced to 20 years imprisonment. His companion, Brigitte Monhaupt, managed to escape.

4. Christian Klar last seen in August 1977 when, with Willy Peter Stoll and Adelheid Schultz they posed as a television crew. They chartered a helicopter to make an aerial reconnaissance of maximum security prisons in southwestern Germany.

5. Angelika Speitel, captured after a shootout with police in Dortmend which left both Speitel and her companion, Michael Knoll, badly wounded. Knoll's brother, Peter Hans Knoll, was also a 2 June Movement member, and on Germany's most wanted list.

A West German judge in Duesseldorf sentenced Angelika Speitel on November 30, 1979 to two life prison terms for her part in the death of a policeman and the wounding of another in 1978. She screamed at the sentence and kicked and bit her guards. About fifty spectators inside the courtroom applauded when she shouted that the revolution would continue.

6. Willy Peter Stoll. On September 6, 1978, while in a restaurant in Dusseldorf with Adelheid Schultz, Stoll was

recognized and the police were alerted. The reason for his recognition were numerous wanted posters which had been circulated and shown on television. The recognition was made even though Stoll had changed from his former hippie-like appearance to a suit and tie. When the police arrived Stoll reached for his gun and was shot and killed. Schultz eluded police and escaped.

Other members of the 2 June Movement are:

1. Michael Bauman, one of Germany's most sought after terrorists and in hiding. In talking with the press Baumann revealed part of the 2 June Movement's Italian connection. Baumann said that he had written part of his memoirs as a terrorist in a 2 June Movement hideaway in Italy. He also revealed that he, like other 2 June members, received money from Giangiacomo Feltrinelli, a wealthy Italian publisher. Feltrinelli, a mysterious figure of the Italian radical left, was an admirer of Fidel Castro and reportedly helped finance the radical Italian group. He and his wife, Inge, hosted Klaus Rainer Rohl, the publisher of *Konkret* and his wife, Ulrike Meinhoff, in their villa in the south of France. Feltrinelli died mysteriously, leaving doubt whether he died trying to put a bomb in place or whether terrorists chose this method to assassinate him. His twisted body was found on March 14, 1972 at the base of a sabotaged electric power pylon on the outskirts of Milan.

2. Petra Schelm, a friend of Bauman's, broke through a Hamburg police blockade on July 1971, and continued on foot. While shooting at the police, she was killed.

3. Angela Luther, at large.

4. Thomas Wiessbecker, believed to be at large.

5. Georg von Rauch, killed by the police on December 6, 1971.

6. Ulrich Schmucker, killed by 2 June Movement on the belief he was an informer.

7. Gotz Tilgener, killed by 2 June Movement on the belief he was an informer.

The Revolutionary Cells

The third German terrorist organization is the Revolutionary Cells. The following is its chronology of terror:

1. March 2, 1974: Firebombed a cathedral in Hamburg.
2. June 12, 1974: Chilean Consulate in West Germany bombed.
3. March 4, 1975: Federal court in Karlsruhe bombed.
4. December 21, 1975: In a combined operation, involving at least three different terrorist groups, six terrorists seized the OPEC offices in Vienna. The seizure was planned by Wadi Haddad of the PFLP. The leader of the hit team was "Carlos" in the hire of Wadi Haddad. Two members of the hit team were from the 2 June Movement, Gabriele Kroecher-Tiedemann and Hans-Joachim Klein, and the remainder were from the PFLP. Later, when Klein defected from the 2 June Movement, he said four terrorists from the Revolutionary Cells were in Vienna and provided the operations support to the hit team. Klein opined that the Revolutionary Cells are the most underrated of all terrorist groups. The reason they were brought into the OPEC operation, he said, was that Wadi Haddad paid the Revolutionary Cells a subsidy of $3,000 to $5,000 a month. Haddad decided he wanted to get something for this money, a significant revelation about the extent of the interconnections between terrorist movements.

One of the reasons that Klein gave up his terrorist life was because the German terrorist movement was no longer independent. It was dependent upon Wadi Haddad and the PFLP. Every decision made by the German terrorists had to be approved by the PFLP. The reasons for this dependence were: 1) The weapons of the German terrorists were supplied by the Palestinian terrorists; 2) The German terrorists needed a place of sanctuary when pursued by the Western European police forces. Only the Palestinians with their sanctuaries in the Near East could provide this.

In return for the money, the weapons, and the sanctuary, the Palestinians received favors such as German gunmen to participate in terrorist acts. Examples are:

A) The Revolutionary Cells were the first European terrorist movement to have liaison with the Palestinian terrorist groups. Wilfried Boese, the chief of the Revolutionary Cells, met the Black September commando group when they arrived in Munich to commit the Olympic massacre. Note that while the primary source of contact between the Revolutionary Cells and the Palestinian terrorist groups was Wadi Haddad and the PFLP, the Black September organization which staged the Munich Massacre was the terrorist offshoot of the El Fatah, a branch of the PLO.

B) The OPEC incident.

C) The hijacking the Air France flight in Athens leading to the Entebbe incident.

Klein said that Boese was the one who nicknamed "Carlos." Carlos it is known preferred the nickname "Johnny." After Boese was killed in Entebbe, Carlos tried to take over the Revolutionary Cells but could not do so.

5. May 15, 1976: Appeals Court in Mann bombed.
6. May 11, 1977: Federal judge's car bombed in Berlin.
7. May 31, 1978: American Arms Hotel in Wiesbaden bombed.

It is evident the modus operandi of the Revolutionary Cells differs from the tactics of the Baader-Meinhoff Gang and the 2 June Movement. First, the Revolutionary Cells are more sophisticated in tradecraft, security and compartmentation, making them an elusive quarry to pursue. Secondly, the targets selected by the Revolutionary Cells were buildings, places and things rather than people. Therefore the targeting appears more in concordance with communist party targets rather than the attack upon people as made by the foco-minded Baader-Meinhoff Gang and the 2 June Movement. Wilfried Boese, aka "Bennie," was later killed at Entebbe.

The Socialist Lawyer's Collective

The three West German terrorist organizations (the Baader-Meinhoff Gang, the 2 June Movement, and the Revolutionary Cells) were supported inside Germany by a conclave of lawyers which grew out of the Socialist Lawyer's Collective organized by Horst Mahler. The collective recruited young Germans into the terrorist's ranks, indoctrinated them, planned their missions, and carried messages and weapons inside the prisons where they were confined. Some of these lawyers are:

1. Siegfried Haag, who was charged with complicity in providing weapons used by the Baader-Meinhoff Gang in its assault on the West German Embassy in Stockholm. He was also identified as an instructor in a Palestinian training camp of Wadi Haddad in the People's Democratic Republic of Yemen where he used the alias "Khaled." Haag was arrested on November 30, 1975 while armed and in possession of documents linking him with "Carlos."

2. Monika Berberich, a member of the Socialist's Lawyer's Collective and an associate of Horst Mahler. Imprisoned for terrorist activities.

3. Horst Mahler, founder of the Socialist Lawyer's Collective. Sentenced to fourteen years imprisonment for terrorist activities in 1972.

4. Roland Mayer, an accomplice of Siegfried Haag.

5. Kurt Groenewald, indicted as being a communication center for the Red Army Faction, passing messages to and from the various terrorists confined in German prisons.

6. Klaus Croissant, imprisoned in West Germany after his extradition from France where he had fled to avoid prosecution. The writ of extradition charged that Croissant's law office was used as a command center for every major terrorist action of recent years involving West Germans. A search of his office uncovered the original declaration used in the "Holger Meins Commando" seizure of the West German Embassy in Stockholm; the "Ulrike Meinhoff Commando" declaration used after the suicide of Meinhoff; the declaration used in conjunction with the murder of

Siegfried Buback; and taped conversations with Palestinian terrorists.

7. Jorg Lang, an associate of Croissant, is reported to be the new head of the Red Army Faction.

8. Armin Newerla, who smuggled explosives into the Stammheim prison.

Petra Krause and Swiss Terrorism

A web of contacts and liaisons between German terrorists and other terrorist groups spread throughout Europe and the Near East. It was difficult to distinguish where the activities of one group ended and the other began. A case in point is the terrorist group headed by Petra Krause, a West German national, in Switzerland.

The terrorist activities of the Krause group are as follows:

1. January — April 1974: Swiss military depots robbed of weapons and explosives.

2. June 18, 1974: Zurich office of U.S. Manufacturer's Hanover Bank was mistakenly bombed. The terrorists thought it was a German bank.

3. September 1973: Italian Consulate in Zurich bombed.

4. January 1975: West German mission to United Nations in Geneva bombed. The explosive used, *Gombam,* had been stolen in Grenoble, France.

Several other West German nationals belonged to the Krause organization. Two of them were Daniel von Arb and Elizabeth von Dyck. When the Krause organization was cracked open by the Swiss police it was found that on two occasions or more von Arb sold Siegfried Haag weapons stolen from Swiss military depots between January and April 1974. Whenever Haag made such purchases he was accompanied by von Dyck. Strangely, evidence was uncovered which showed that Krause acted under orders she received from Haag.

European Terrorist Connections

The weapons and explosives stolen by the Krause organization and those purchased by Haag have turned up throughout Europe. Some were captured with the Baader-Meinhoff members. Explosives found on them consisted of grenades as well as anti-tank and anti-personnel mines. Explosives found by the Spanish police on the Catalan Express, bringing arms into Spain for the Grupo Resistencia Antifascista Fundado el Primero de Octubre (GRAPO), were from the same stock. At least one pistol used by the Japanese Red Army in the seizure of the French Embassy in the Hague was traced to the Baader-Meinhoff Gang.

Moukarbel—Carlos' PFLP chief in Paris—had been in Zurich, Switzerland where he met with Petra Krause. He had three missions: 1) to buy grenades and mines, which Krause's organization had stolen from the Swiss Army depots; 2) to arrange for the transit of the Japanese Red Army group to France and on to the Netherlands to seize the French Embassy in the Hague; and 3) to recruit the Petra Krause organization to join the PFLP group in Paris with Carlos. The Petra Krause organization refused because, although they robbed, they were not ready to murder as they knew Moukarbel and Carlos wanted them to do.

The Krause organization was a connecting link between German and Italian terrorists. One meeting place for German and Italian terrorists was the Eco-Libro bookstore in Zurich. Close contact was maintained by the Red Brigades with Petra Krause. After she was arrested the Red Brigades sent support members to case the Winterthur Prison where she was held to determine whether or not it would be possible to arrange a jailbreak. It proved unnecessary. Through a number of legal manuevers, Petra Krause is now free and residing in Italy.

Similar to the happenings in Switzerland, a series of terrorists acts in Vienna also led back into the German terror machine. On November 9, 1977 an Austrian businessman, Walter Michael Palmers, was kidnapped by terrorists and released after the payment of 1.9 million dollars in assorted currencies. It was an unusual case in that internal terrorist released the kidnap victim who might have been able to identify them. However, the money was so great a sum that the terrorists were willing to take the risk. The first break in the case came when two Austrian students, Thomas Gratt and Othmar Keplinger, were arrested while trying to cross the frontier into Italy. They were found to have in their possession $115,000 of the money paid in the Palmers kidnapping.

On interrogation Gratt and Keplinger confirmed the participation of West German terrorists in the Viennese operation; also that a mutual support base was located in Udine, Italy. They also revealed that three West German female terrorists were in Vienna during the Palmers kidnapping.

A month later, on December 14, 1977, the Austrian police arrested a West German female, Waltraud Boock, in Vienna for attempted bank robbery. Her accomplices were her husband, Peter Juergen Boock, and Rold Klemens Wagner. A pistol found in their possession was traced to Christian Klar, a 2 June Movement member on the wanted list for the Buback murder. Klar had purchased the gun in Italy. At the time of purchase he was with Sabine Schmitz, an associate of Siegfried Haag. The web connected the Socialist Lawyer's Collective and Haag and Croissant.

On October 6, 1978 the Vienna police located the apartment referred to almost a year before by Gratt and Keplinger and verified that it had been used by three female German terrorists; Inge Viett, Ingrid Siepmann, and Ingrid Barabasz. Viett was a 2 June Movement member, closely associated with its chief, Ralf Reinders. Siepmann, also a 2 June Movement terrorist, spent a year in a Palestinian training camp. Barabasz had previously been arrested with terrorist Christian Moeller, but both were released. Subsequent to his release, Moeller was again arrested, this time in Switzerland in the company of Gabriele Kroecher-Tiedemann. It was found that Kroecher also had currency from the Palmer kidnapping in her possession. Both Kroecher and Moeller received twenty year sentences.

Additional liaisons between German and Italian terrorists were shown when a Chilean, Aldo Orlando Marin Pinones, blew himself up while planting a bomb in Turin, Italy. Marin had entered Italy from Cuba. In checking his antecedents it was found that Marin roomed with another Chilean, Juan Teofilio Paillacar, who had also entered Italy from Cuba. Investigation after the arrest of Norbert Kroecher, the architect of the abortive kidnap plot in Sweden and the husband of Gabriele Kroecher-Tiedemann, revealed that Kroecher had the name and address of Paillacar in his possession. This discovery indicated a German-Italian and possibly Cuban connection.

Nor was the Netherlands neglected. Luduina Janssen, the member of the Red Help terrorist organization in the Netherlands, confessed that Red Help had contacts with the PFLP and the Baader-Meinhoff gang.

Dissolution of the W. German Terrorists

Beginning in December 1977, with the arrest of Gabriele Kroecher-Tiedemann and Christian Moeller in Switzerland, the coming months were hard ones for the German terrorist movement. Stefan Wisniewski was arrested in Paris. Peter Juergen Boock, Sieglinde Hoffman, Brigitte Monhaupt, and Rolf Clemens Wagner were arrested in Zagreb, Yugoslavia. Marion Folkerts was arrested in Paris. Till Myer, Gabriele Rollnik, Gudrun Stuermer, and Angelika Goder were arrested in Varna, Bulgaria. Astrid Proll was apprenhended in London, England, where she worked as an auto mechanic. Angelika Speitel and Michael Knoll were arrested by the German police in Dortmund; Knoll resisted and was killed. The toll was a great one with many others such as Siegfried Haag, Klaus Croissant, and Klaus Mahler in jail; and Andreas Baader, Ulrike Meinhoff, and Gudrun Ensslin dead.

On July 16, 1978 Kristina Berster was arrested by U.S. officials near Burlington, Vermont as she tried to cross the border into the United States from Canada. When arrested she was using a stolen Iranian passport. The passport belonged to Shahrzad S. Nobari. It was stolen by students belonging to the Confederation of Iranian Students, National Union (CISNU) during a sit-in of the Iranian Consulate in Geneva, Switzerland. Berster provided U.S. authorities with details about Miss Nobari's family and life, trying to prove that she was Nobari. It evidenced that CISNU members briefed Berster on the legend to use in conjunction with the passport. The connection between the Iranian students and the Baader-Meinhoff gang was further confirmed after the fall of the shah. On December 18, 1979 Hassan Sans, the former deputy chief of the Iranian security service, SAVAK, was interviewed in his prison cell in Teheran. He said that since contact existed between the Iranian students and the Baader-Meinhoff gang, SAVAK cooperated very closely with German intelligence services and provided the Germans with relevant information.

Disillusionment and disenchantment then set into the terrorist ranks. *Konkret* publisher Klaus Rainer Rohl became frightened at the anarchy he had helped spawn. In his autobiography, Rohl wrote that he and Ulrike Meinhoff were secret members of the communist party and that the Soviets had funded *Konkret* in the amount of $400,000. Horst Mahler himself publicly condemned terror. Reportedly, even "Carlos" left the terrorist ranks. Hans-Joachim Klein, who was with "Carlos" in the OPEC raid, said "Carlos" was paid off handsomely, presumably by the Libyans, and wrote his resignation to Wadi Haddad. The Baader-Meinhoff Gang, inside their prison cells, fought with each other. The central issue was whether terrorists should kill people or whether it was better to destroy things. Baader, the advocate of the Foco theory, saw nothing wrong in killing people since it was germane to the revolution. Karl-Heina Dellwo took exception. He wrote, "Euphoria and admiration of the Palestine Liberation Front had taken the place of ideas among the Germans with the result that many sympathizers had been alienated and the Red Army Faction's moral claim had been jeopardized."

The Foco theory failed in Germany. It failed because the terrorists could not intensify the program of terrorism to the point that it could create a loss in the people's confidence toward their government. Secondly, the Foco theory failed because of good police work. The following factors were, I believe, the elements of this effective police work:

1. The German police remained in relentless pursuit of the terrorists in much the same way the Bolivian army pursued Che Guevara. The terrorists could not rest or reorganize. They were fugitives and remained on the run.
2. Special terrorist units were formed in each police force in the same way that the Brazilians had organized "CODI," the counterterrorist organization. The policemen working against the terrorists became experts in the field. They knew their enemy intimately, their backgrounds, their families, their mistresses and paramours, their likes and dislikes, and their strengths and weaknesses.
3. The German police "wanted" lists and poster campaigns were a great success.

The German people were not yet terrorized and did not fear informing on a terrorist, in contrast with Cuba, Iran, and Italy. As a policeman remarked in Brazil, "The terrorist is a fish in an alien sea." It was certainly true in Germany. Andreas Baader, Ulrike Meinhoff,

Gudrun Ensslin and the others swam as fish in an alien sea of millions of other people who were repulsed by terror. With efficient police work and the help of the people the terrorists were netted. Even the communist parties and Marxist-Leninist splinter groups disowned the Baader-Meinhoff Gang. Even Mahler concluded violence was not the way to a successful revolution.

7
Terrorist Propaganda

Terrorists regard the press as an ally because it propagandizes their acts of terrorism, helping terrorize the citizenry and achieve their political objective. However, in the case of Che Guevara the linkage between the terrorist and publicity backfired. Because the Bolivian government wanted to avoid publicity, Guevara was executed rather than taken before a tribunal.

A short time before the Bolivian army found Guevara, he was joined by his friend and journalist, Regis Debray, the author of *Revolution In A Revolution.* While they were together the Bolivian army found Guevara and began its dogged pursuit. Guevara was confident he could lose his pursuers and he and his band, with Debray in tow, fled. Later they separated. Debray took the road to La Paz and Guevara and his band plunged deeper into the wilderness.

Debray was arrested and jailed before he reached La Paz. He was charged with revolutionary conspiracy and later brought to trial. Had the Bolivian government known that Debray was a leftist celebrity in intellectual European circles, it might have treated him differently by quietly deporting him to France. But his notoriety remained unknown until 300 international journalists arrived in La Paz to cover his trial. They reported favorably on Debray and derogatorily on the Bolivian government. With the deluge of unfavorable publicity the Bolivian regime felt its stability threatened. Therefore, when Guevara was captured, the Bolivian government did not want to risk a public trial. They reasoned that if 300 reporters arrived to cover Debray's trial, ten times that number would probably come to Guevara's trial.

The government was also apprehensive that a trial would become a political forum for Guevara and he would become a martyr to future revolutionaries. It felt there was no alternative but to use a quite common military prerogative in Latin America and execute Guevara as a captured guerrilla, which he was. The order of execution was given.

In a short time the field commander radioed that the order had been carried out and Guevara was dead. He was then instructed to fingerprint the corpse so there would be no question that Guevara had been executed. The commander replied he had anticipated the request and had severed Guevara's hands and would bring them to La Paz in a jar of embalming fluid. An attempt was also made to embalm Guevara's body, but the soldiers-turned-embalmers forgot to patch the bullet holes and the fluid ran out of the open wounds.

Several months later Antonio Arguedas, the Minister of Defense who helped track Guevara, defected to Cuba and took the hands with him.

However, terror brings terror and the terror which surrounded Guevara continues. Those who hunted him down are now in turn being hunted and killed by Guevara's supporters. On May 11, 1976 General Joaquin Zenteno Anaya, who was in charge of the miltiary region where Guevara was killed on October 8, 1967, was murdered on a street in Paris, where he was the Bolivian ambassador. A terrorist organization, the Che Guevara International Brigade, took credit for the murder. A month later, on June 2, 1976 Bolivian ex-president Juan Jose Torres, who also was involved in Guevara's capture, was killed in Buenos Aires by a barrage of bullets.

Armed Propaganda

Carlos Marighella wrote in the *Mini-Manual,* "The coordination of urban guerrilla actions, including each armed action, is the principal way of making armed propaganda.

"These actions, carried out with specific and determined objectives, inevitably become propaganda material for the mass communications systems.

"Bank assaults, ambushes, desertions, and diverting of arms, the rescue of prisoners, executions, kidnappings, sabotage, terrorism and the war of nerves are all cases in point.

"Airplanes diverted in flight by revolutionary actions, moving ships and trains assaulted and seized by guerrillas, can also be solely for propaganda effect."

The result of armed propaganda is that the more daring and gruesome the terrorism act is, the greater the publicity. Simply stated, the objective of terrorist propaganda is to terrorize. Marighella understood this well when he wrote:

"It is enough to win the support of a part of the people and this can be done by popularizing the following slogan, 'Let he who does not wish to do anything for the revolutionaries do nothing against them.'"

Execution is an effective form of armed propaganda. Shortly after Fidel Castro took refuge in the Sierra Maestra Mountains, the peasants were called together and the richest landowner of the area was shot and killed in front of them. It was a terror tactic dating from primitive times. The king was dead, a new king was in power.

Adherents of this concept of "armed propaganda" point to the fact that while Castro was in the Sierra Maestra Mountains he did not have a single political rally. All of his propaganda was based upon "armed propaganda."

Outside of such "armed propaganda" publicized by the mass communication system, terrorist propaganda in flysheets and manifestos have been uniformly poorly written, lacking a message, and written in a hodgepodge of Marxisms. The terrorists make no effort to improve their writing, instead focusing on "armed propaganda" because it is terror that makes a revolution. If the terrorist is daring, innovative, and brutal, "armed propaganda" will be headline news. A case which meets all of the criteria was the assassination of the President of Spain, Admiral Luis Carrero Blanco, by Basque terrorists on December 20, 1973.

Carrero was selected as the victim when the terrorists almost casually learned he was a man of fixed habit, a churchgoer who attended the Church of San Francisco de Borja in Madrid each morning at nine o'clock. A casing team confirmed the information. Each morning Carrero's car, and the escort car of bodyguards, snaked through the narrow streets of Madrid to take him to church and then on to his office. The terrorists found it hard to believe that an official as powerful as Carrero left himself so vulnerable to attack.

They made their plans, first to kidnap him, but later changed the plan to assassination. A basement apartment was rented along Carrero's route and from it the terrorists tunneled thirty feet under the sidewalk and street until they were directly under the place where Carrero's car passed each day. They piled in 165 pounds of dynamite and triggered the explosion on signal from a distance of 100 yards, using an electric detonator.

The explosion was tremendous with the entire concentrated force of the blast moving upward. Carrero's car disappeared from sight. His bodyguards, following closely behind, thought Carrero's driver had sped through the blast and was far ahead of them. Instead Carrero's car was blown five stories high and landed on the other side of the roof of the church. There, it ricocheted and fell over the side of the church away from the street and came to rest on a second floor terrace. Several hours passed before the car was found, because no one thought of looking on the other side of the church. An instant after the explosion, however, the terrorists escaped, shouting that gas had exploded. It was "armed propaganda" that made headline news.

JRA Propaganda

The Japanese Red Army (JRA) devised a double propaganda tactic. During June 1978 the JRA sent letters to the passengers who had been hostages on Japan Airline flight 474, which the JRA had hijacked in September 1977. In addition to their terror from being hijacked, the victims were terrorized a second time by being informed they were on a terrorist mailing list. The letter read:

"To the Japanese people, comrades and friends, the Japanese Red Army in commemoration of the sixth anniversay of the 30 May Lod Airport struggle, appeals for solidarity in the name of all commandos of the army. . . . We, members of the Japanese Red Army pledge to fight to the last through solidarity."

It was a repetition of Marighella's threat: "Let he who does not wish to do anything for the revolutionaries do nothing against them."

Chinese Communist Propaganda

The organization of the Chinese People's Army has built-in "armed propaganda" which is controlled by the communist party. The basic Chinese guerrilla unit is a group of three. Three groups of three make a squad. Three squads make a platoon, four platoons a company, and five companies a batallion. One member of each group of three is a communist party member. Each squad therefore has three party members. A platoon has nine. All of the communists in the units which comprise a company form a base organization or cell. At batallion level a committee is formed, and through this organizational process communist control extends from top to bottom. It prevents military uprisings and political differences, since dissension is dealt with before it can become a force. The Chinese believe their military forces must remain pure in revolutionary spirit because the army is the social consciousness of the communist party.

From this structure the communist party members in the army form political teams and fashion "armed propaganda." One method is through the People's Revolutionary Tribunals. When the guerrilla army expands its zone of operations, communist political teams go into the enlarged zone to propagandize the people. The first point of contact is the party members who are residents in the zone. With their help contact is established with the non-communist residents. The mission of the political team is to convince the people that the guerrilla army is their army and their friend. One terror tactic is implemented through the People's Revolutionary Tribunal. The political teams arrest the area's largest landowner. It does not matter who he is or what he has done. He may be good or bad but it will be found, by one means or another, that somewhere, somehow in the past, he has wronged someone.

The political teams ask the people to denounce the landowner. In the end someone always does and it opens up the door to real and fictitious denouncements. After they are submitted and compiled the severity of the landowner's crimes is apparent to all. A People's Revolutionary Tribunal is convened with the intention of finding the defendant guilty and he is summarily executed. His land is parceled out to the peasants in agrarian reform style, showing how it will be in the future under communist rule. It is enough to win over the peasants.

When government forces try to recapture the area, the peasants join the guerrilla army, because they know if the government force is successful the land will be taken away from them and given to the legal owners. The peasants now have the land and are ready to fight to keep it. This is "armed propaganda," too.

Mao Tse Tung said, "Every Communist must grasp the truth, political power grows out of the barrel of a gun."

8
Fighting Terrorists

Terrorists believe their political cause is just and are irretrievably uncomprising in this belief. They are not interested in moderation and despise and hate those who oppose them. During 1958 in Santiago de Cuba, the police shot a young terrorist caught in an act of sabotage. The wound, a rifle bullet in the stomach, was critical, and one of the policemen tried to comfort the terrorist. The dying youth rejected the aid and spat at the policeman. The officer could not understand why the terrorist hated him so.

Hate, coupled with the lust for a political goal makes the terrorist a killer, an enemy of society. It is not enough only to protect ourselves from terrorists; we must fight back and destroy them in the same way we make society safe from criminals.

Terrorist Characteristics

Terrorists are very much alike. There is little difference between the terrorists of Iran and those of Italy or Germany. There are four characteristics which terrorists worldwide have in common:

1. They are young.
2. They are educated.
3. They are middle to upper-middle class.
4. They are Marxist-Leninist.

The dominant mutual characteristic is class origin because from this base it follows that its members are educated in colleges or universities. They are exposed to a new political approach, leftist and Marxist-Leninist, which they absorb, and then succumb to recruitment by terrorist leaders.

Of 24 German students who turned terrorist, 21 were high school and college dropouts. Of 40 terrorists "wanted" by the German authorities 24, or 60 percent of the total were women.

Terrorists worldwide are young in age and form the nuclei or "foco" for urban terrorism to create a state of chaos. As the chaos deepens and a revolutionary situation nears, older people join them because of political or economic factors or fear of terrorism and counterterrorism. A dissident political base is established and it becomes a fertile recruiting ground for terrorist organizations. Uruguay is a case in point. The Uruguayan economic situation deteriorated until there were more educated people than there were jobs for them.

Doctors, engineers and other professionals were recruited into the ranks of the Tupamaros, which became onc of thc most efficient and skillful terrorist organizations of the century.

Education is required to understand political doctrine. Rarely have laborers, farmers, or other blue collar workers joined terrorist organizations. They have neither the time nor the political motivation to be a terrorist. Their time is spent in work, not conspiracy. Terrorists are uniformly from the middle class. Yet rarely are terrorists businessmen, or employers producing a product. They are from the segment which leans toward academia—the chic political left of coffee houses which gave birth to the Baader-Meinhoff gang in West Germany.

The Baader-Meinhoff gang provides an interesting example of the general abstinence of blue collar workers from urban terrorism. Trying to reach down into the masses, the Baader-Meinhoff gang recruited two blue collar workers, Karl Ruhland and Rolf Mauer. After their recruitment, however, they were treated as subordinates. They became second class revolutionaries and performed only menial tasks such as maintaining the gang's automobiles. When Ruhland and Mauer were captured by the police they confessed they knew little, and cared less, about the political doctrine preached at them by the other gang members.

A Brazilian police inspector commented upon the youthful nature of urban terrorists, "The greatest enemies of terrorism are graduation and marriage." He was right but failed to take into account that terrorists are criminals. Once they have killed or kidnapped, not even graduation or marriage can separate them from the terrorist gang to which they are irrevocably chained. Terrorist leaders know and exploit this fact. New recruits are quickly sent into action. They commit a crime and it becomes impossible to return to their former lives, even more so with each additional act of terror they commit. In the end the members of a terrorist organization become bound to each other. This is the exact end result the terrorist leader wants. He has built a group of skilled terrorists, wanted by the police and unable to return to their former lives.

It is difficult for the police to approach terrorists for intelligence or information purposes. A communist, for example, is far easier to approach because unlike the terrorist he is not a common criminal who has killed, kidnapped, or maimed. It is this inherent criminality which makes dangerous any kind of an approach to the terrorist. If he has killed he believes he has done so with justification. In his eyes his acts are moralistic. He may kill when approached by anyone. "Carlos," for example, killed two detectives who came to his apartment not to arrest him but only to talk with him.

Terrorist Membership

Terrorist groups are generally without popular support and are small in number. A few rare exceptions occur when a terrorist group becomes amalgamated within a national front organization such as the People's Strugglers and the People's Sacrifice Guerrillas in Iran.

The Popular Front for the Liberation of Palestine has a membership of about 500 people, but this is mainly a political representation. When activists are needed it recruits terrorists from one of many refugee camps. The Japanese Red Army, on the other hand, has only 30 members but all of them are active terrorists, capable of committing murder. The same is true of the Baader-Meinhoff gang in West Germany with a membership of 50 activists and 300 active sympathizers. In the Netherlands the Red Cell organization has 25 members. Again, they are activists. Surviving members of the Revolutionary Coordinating Council (JCR) in the Southern cone of Latin America may number 500, including support members.

The larger terrorist units are rural guerrilla forces such as the New People's Army (NPA) in the Philippines with about 1,000 members and the Revolutionary Armed Forces of Colombia (FARC) with 800 to 1,000 members. The Guerrilla forces of the Guerrilla Army of the Poor (EGP) in Guatemala number about 125 and the Sandinist National Liberation Front (FSLN) in Nicaragua had about 125 activists. Later, however, in the fall of 1978 and on into 1979 the FSLN achieved its objective and brought a full-bloom insurgency into being in Nicaragua. The peoplc bcgan to take sides. The poor were recruited into the National Guard and the middle class youths flocked to the revolutionary side, swelling the ranks of the FSLN.

It is difficult to arrive at accurate estimates of terrorist strength because eyewitnesses to terrorist actions are nervous or panic-stricken, and estimates are exaggerated. One rule of thumb method is to divide eyewitness reports by four and adjust downward. For example, where there are reports that 100 guerrillas of a national liberation movement ambushed an army patrol, my experience has shown that 18 to 20 guerrillas is a more accurate number.

There are a considerable number of pharmacists recruited by terrorist groups because of the need for first aid treatment, drugs, and medicines. A terrorist organization without a medical connection is vulnerable. When Consul Curtis Cutter rammed his way out of a road block in Porto Alegre, Brazil, he ran over a terrorist and broke his leg. The man was in extreme pain. Because the terrorists did not have a medical connection, they were forced to take him to a hospital where he was promptly arrested and interrogated. In a matter of hours the whole gang was under arrest. Carlos Marighella wrote, "In no circumstances can the wounded urban guerrilla be abandoned at the site of the battle or left to the enemy's hands."

Church Support of Terrorism

Two main centers of support for urban terrorism exist. One is the university. The other is the church, both Protestant and Catholic. The role of the university in revolutionary matters is well known, but the reasons why church elements support revolutions are more abstruse. In Cuba the Franciscan Order supported Castro. In the Dominican Republic, the Dominican Order was in support of Francisco Caamamo, and in Brazil the Dominican Order supported Marighella. Also in Brazil and Guatemala, the Protestant church supported revolution until the church leaders were ordered out of the country.

A guerrilla leader told me the reasons behind the Catholic involvement in revolutionary activities, as it was explained to him in the Chinese guerrilla school in Nanking. It seems that shortly after World

War II the Vatican saw Eastern Europe fall to the communists. The theoreticians foresaw a rise in world population, along with an ever-increasing food shortage problem. They reasoned world revolution was inevitable, and that if the church did not become involved in leading the coming revolution, the church would also be swept under. The Chinese believed they could work with the church on limited political objectives but the church could not be given a leadership role. They believed the church was motivated by its own interests, because it was to the church's advantage to prevent total revolution and complete change in the economic and social spheres.

Now the Church's involvement in Latin revolutionary activities has grown to the extent that the Vatican hierarchy believes it has gotten out of hand. An estimated two-thirds of all Catholic priests and nuns in Latin America are Marxists who support terrorism and insurgency. They advocate what is called the "Liberation Theology." It preaches that Jesus Christ was a revolutionary and demands the state ownership and control of all means of production of goods, energy, transportation and education with the objective of establishing a government patterned after Castro's Cuba.

The "Liberation Theology" has become one of the insurgents most powerful weapons. As Bishop Mendez Arceo of Cuernavaca, Mexico, has declared, "The Kingdom of Heaven can come about in our day only by Marxism."

Seven hundred million Roman Catholics live in Latin America and most are the uneducated poor. They kneel and pray in church, and their priest tells them that Marxism is the path to the Kingdom of Heaven. The poor believe it is true because it was told to them by a man of God.

So serious is the threat to the existing order that Pope John Paul II went to Mexico to open the Third General Conference of Latin American Bishops (CELAM) in the city of Puebla on January 29, 1979. The Pope delivered the Vatican's policy. There would be, he said, no compromise with the Marxists, no mixture of politics with religion, no armed insurgency, and no political activity by the clergy. Above all, he disputed that Jesus Christ was a revolutionary whose purpose, as extolled in the Liberation Theology, was to liberate the masses from capitalism. The bishops listened but said little.

Time has shown that the Pope's statement made little impact upon Bishop Mendez and others such as Archibishop Romero of Nicaragua. For instance, the Catholic church remained in the forefront of the insurgency in Nicaragua. In the fall of 1979 the Nicaraguan Sandinist government had largely installed a Cuban-type government in Nicaragua, including 4,000 block informant committees. Yet the Catholic clerics of Nicaragua issued a pastoral letter affirming their loyalty to the Liberation Theology.

In Brazil, on the advice of the United States and the Catholic Church, the government authorized the return of communists who had been in exile for fifteen years. Luis Carlos Prestes,, the secretary general of the Brazilian Communists Party (PCB), spoke at a rally in the Lapa section of Sao Paulo after his return from exile. He said that the Catholic Church is the best ally of the communists, stating that the Catholic Church is "the most progressive in the world, including most of its hierarchy" and that "today religion is no longer a basic issue for the PCB—we are no longer atheists."

In the Basque region of Spain, the Catholic priests are highly nationalistic and support the Basque terror organizations even though it is Marxist-Leninist. For instance, one priest publicly urged Christians to adopt Marxist thinking. He said, "There are many Christians who live their Christianity through Marxism."

Carlos Marighella wrote, "The priest who is an urban guerrilla is an active ingredient in the ongoing Brazilian revolutionary war, and constitutes a powerful arm in the struggle against military power and North American Imperialism."

Terrorist Training

Terrorists are not trained professionally. With the exception of those who go to a training school in the Mideast or Cuba, most terrorists learn by doing. Even though a terrorist depends upon weaponry, they have little practice in weaponry, because there are few places where a terrorist can practice without being arrested. In September 1978 the police at Dortmund, Germany surprised three terrorists at target practice in a forest. The police wounded and captured two of them in an ensuing gunfight. The Baader-Meinhoff Gang, on the other hand, practiced shooting near airports where the sound of the aircraft muted the gunfire. Therefore, terrorists are not the best marksmen. A businessman given a moderate training program in weaponry and marksmanship can generally be assured that, in case of a showdown with a terrorist, he will likely be the better marksman.

The same weaknesses apply in other facets of the terrorist's professionalism. Again it is because he does not have the formal training given to police and security officers. Few terrorists, for example, have the steadfast discipline drummed into them needed to maintain a secure, clandestine life. Sooner or later, many will take the easy way and make a mistake. Terrorists have the same weakness they look for in their victims. The terrorist also fails to vary his routine, because routine is strongly rooted in every person. A terrorist may arrange a risky meeting with another terrorist. If the meeting occurs without incident, his inclination is to hold his next meeting in the same place rather than finding and testing a new location. The same adherence to routine also applies to hotels where the terrorist may stay or bars, restaurants, and coffee houses he may frequent. He returns to places where he was previously safe.

We have learned that when a terrorist meeting place is known, he might return there. Therefore, such meeting places must be surveilled; if not, an inside informer must be recruited. This is routine counterintelligence work.

As terrorists try to hide, going from one strata of society to another, they carry tell-tale signs of their middle class, university background with them. They are noticed by the people who surround them, and it is more difficult to hide than they thought. A member of the Baader-Meinhoff Gang said, "Eating food with your hands in one restaurant may be as noticeable as eating a sandwich with a knife and fork in another."

For example, three top leaders of the Cuban 26 of July Movement, Armando Hart, Antonio Buch, and Javier Pazos, left the Sierra Maestro Mountains in January of 1958, after meeting with Fidel Castro. Disguised as farmers, they went to the city of Bayamo where they boarded a train for Santiago de Cuba. Within several minutes they were arrested by a suspicious policeman. The tell-tale sign that tipped off the officer was their muddy shoes. No Cuban campasino would board a train or go to the city with muddy shoes.

Neatness was their custom, but the underground leaders did not know this.

Through the use of the block informant system, authoritarian governments are very successful in finding people who try to hide. Each city block has at least one recruited informant who knows everything about everyone in the block. Anyone who is spending more money than he should be for his type of employment falls under suspicion immediately. Along these same lines police and security forces place "pickets"—a scattering of informants—to report upon anything suspicious. Pickets are placed or recruited in the local Palestinian community to report on new arrivals or messengers passing through, or anything which appears out of the ordinary.

OBAN

Perhaps the most effective means of fighting terrorism was organized by the Brazilians. Their pioneer counterterrorist organization in Sao Paulo was called "OBAN," an acronym for Operation Badeirantes. OBAN coordinated all police and security activities against Brazil's urban terrorists. It was organized to end jurisdictional disputes between the many civilian and military agencies which were working against the same target. OBAN was made-up of five teams, each headed by a military officer. Team personnel were drawn from all of the civilian and military police and security services in Sao Paulo state. A directive was issued to all police services that every prisoner arrested on suspicion of subversion had to be turned over to OBAN. The directive was vigorously enforced. Consequently, and without exception, prisoners arrested on subversion charges were escorted to OBAN. OBAN not only eliminated the friction and rivalry between the competing security services, but as a positive achievement created a center of counterterrorist expertise. The men who ran OBAN knew for the first time who the terrorists were, their targets, and their modus operandi. OBAN proved so successful that in the fall of 1969, by presidential decree, a similar organization was set up in each state of Brazil. The new nationwide organization was called Internal Defense Operational Commands or "CODI."

CODI was staffed by security personnel from all services, but mainly military men were selected. It was composed of two major sections. One was the intelligence section which had three components. The first was the intelligence unit which kept track of terrorist gangs. Second was the interrogation unit which questioned all prisoners arrested on subversion charges. The third unit reviewed documents, passports, and pocket litter found on those arrested on subversion charges.

The other half of CODI was the operations section. It followed up on leads obtained by the intelligence section, raided suspect terrorist sites, and made arrests.

The way in which OBAN worked was that if the intelligence section uncovered a lead, perhaps an address of a suspect terrorist, it was passed immediately to the operations section. The operation section would then raid the address and arrest the alleged terrorist. The operations officer would next turn over the prisoner to the intelligence section. His interrogation would begin as intelligence checked its files on the suspect. Documentation experts also analyzed any documents the suspect carried, checking for clues. If any leads developed, they were passed to the operation section and the process repeated itself.

Critics charged that CODI used brutal means while interrogating the suspects. Urban terrorists were soon directed by their organizations to resist interrogation for twenty-four hours if arrested. During this time, other affiliated terrorists would become aware of the member's arrest. The terrorists could then hide, clamp down on security, and put compartmentation into effect, minimizing the effect of the arrest.

Consequently, the interrogators sometimes used brutal means to break the prisoner *quickly,* before the terrorists could hide. Here we have one of counterterrorism's great ironies. Police fall under heavy pressure from the public to end the terror, yet if they cannot the public loses faith in the government. Brutal prisoner treatment is one consequence of this pressure. Also, in terrorist situations where terror becomes brutal, it inevitably is met with brutal counterterror.

Hans Joachim Klein, the German terrorist, said of counterterrorist tactics, "Urban guerrilla warfare as a form of struggle has collapsed all over the world. It works only so long as the state that is being fought adheres to some extent to democratic laws. If it resorts to military force and torture any urban guerrilla movement is bound to collapse. Militarily it is hopelessly inferior."

Other Counterterrorist Measures

One of the most brutal anti-hijack measures was used by Ethiopia. Ethiopia was plagued by a number of hijacking incidents. As a deterrent, it organized a sky marshall type of counterforce. Shortly thereafter a hijacker was captured during his unsuccessful attempt to take over an airliner in flight. The sky marshalls evacuated the first class section and tied the hijacker to a seat and gagged him. They then tied blankets around his chest. When that was done, they cut his throat from ear to ear. As the plane continued its flight, the hijacker bled to death, silently with the oozing blood being absorbed by the blanket. The seat and floor remained spotless. At the end of the flight the bloodless corpse was carried out, a grim warning to would-be terrorists that the cost of defeat was death.

A different type of situation happened in Brazil. In cases where the terrorist held hostages and demanded the release of prisoners, Brazil, as a matter of policy, complied with the demands; however, as the released prisoners boarded planes for Algiers or Havana, a security official warned each of them that if he ever again was caught in Brazil, he would be killed. After a short training course in Cuba or Algeria, and newly supplied with money and false passports, some terrorists returned to Brazil to take up where they had left off. Invariably they were eventually detected by the police and killed in the ensuing gunfight.

In 1973 twenty-nine terrorists entered Brazil. The police knew they carried false passports, which in Portuguese slang were called "cold documents." As psychological warfare, when a terrorist was killed in a street fight, the police buried him in the name of his "cold documents." Somehow it struck terror into terrorists, knowing that they would be buried for eternity under a false name; friends, family and other terrorists might never know they had died.

Terrorists and Professionalism

The professionalism of terrorists varies. Those who are internal terrorists, living underground and wanted by the local police, are of a higher professional quality than international terrorists who live in a sanctuary. Those who are constantly wanted by the police learn through necessity to be clandestine. They become more adept at casing, surveillance, the execution of the act of terror, and the escape.

International terrorists who reside in countries where they are not wanted by the police do not acquire the clandestinity and professionalism of internal terrorists.

Terrorist training schools in the Mideast do not provide the kind of training that corrects professional deficiencies. Such schools in the People's Democratic Republic of Yemen and elsewhere are designed to simply give basic training to terrorists who cannot safely train in their own countries. They are "bang and boom" schools, where the students are taught weaponry, target practice, how to make and explode bombs, and elementary guerrilla warfare tactics.

The terrorist acts of the legendary "Carlos" show little professionalism. In London on December 30, 1973 Carlos tried to assassinate Edward Sieff, a wealthy Jew. Carlos chose Sieff's home as the site for the murder. Singlehandedly and unprofessionally, Carlos forced his entry into Sieff's residence at gunpoint. It is not known if he had cased Sieff's home. If so, the casing was either bad or not heeded, because Carlos overlooked the presence of Sieff's wife. She saw Carlos holding a gun on the butler and locked herself in a room where she telephoned the police. Carlos saw her but made no pursuit. He confronted Sieff in the bathroom where he was shaving. Carlos fired one shot at point-blank range which he mistakenly thought was fatal. Why he did not fire again is not known. From an assassin's viewpoint, having already reached the act of murder, it was a mistake. Few assassins have failed at point-blank range as Carlos did.

It is believed that Carlos was the terrorist who on January 25, 1974 threw a homemade bomb into the Israeli Bank of Hapoalin in London. Poorly thrown, the bomb bounced off the floor and landed next to a counter which shielded its blast. Little damage was done.

On September 15, 1974 a terrorist threw a hand grenade into the Drug Store Saint-Germain in Paris. Two people were killed and twenty-five injured. It is believed the terrorist was Carlos, but the act was crude, not the type expected from a renowned international terrorist.

On June 27, 1975 in Paris, Carlos killed two policemen, Jean Donati and Raymond Dous, as well as his own accomplice, Michel Moukarbel. All three had come to Carlos' living quarters unexpected. Carlos thought Moukarbel had talked and the police were there to arrest him. He killed all three and fled. Afterward it appeared Moukarbel had not talked and the police only meant to question Carlos as their guns were not drawn. However, Carlos' impulsiveness resulted in three unnecessary murders.

According to Hans-Joachim Klein, the reason why Carlos killed Moukarbel was not that Carlos thought Moukarbel was an informer. Klein stated that when Carlos killed the two French policemen, Moukarbel was standing in the corner holding his hands over his head. Carlos killed him for being a coward.

Carlos' last big operation was the seizure of the OPEC offices in Vienna on December 21, 1975. It was here he announced, "Tell them I am the famous Carlos." The operation probably can be judged as successful even though one terrorist, Hans-Joachim Klein, was wounded and left behind. It did not appear well-planned, though, and it is extremely doubtful that a prior casing of the OPEC offices took place. The seizure had all of the appearances of a crash operation. When the terrorists reached the OPEC offices they went through the suite opening doors, not knowing what was on the other side, clearly indicating a lack of prior planning.

In total, Carlos lacked professionalism and showed no established modus operandi. Certain of his operational mannerisms, such as staying at expensive hotels, were purely self-indulgent. Nonetheless, Carlos is dangerous because of his ability to kill anyone at any time for any reason. It is the *raison d'etre* of a terrorist and because of this Carlos holds prominence among his peers.

Hans-Joachim Klein reported in September of 1978 that Carlos was paid off by an Arab country (probably Libya) and left the terrorist business. Klein said he was paid not to kill two of the OPEC hostages: the oil minister from Saudi Arabia, Jamani, and Amusegar from Iran. Since Carlos still worked for Wadi Haddad, he thought Haddad would have him killed. But Haddad died a short time later, possibly from cancer.

Psychological Considerations

One difficult aspect of fighting terrorists relates to their psychological make-up. They are unlike ordinary people. It is difficult to foresee or anticipate their next act. I have selected three terrorists to illustrate this point.

The first is Luduina Janssen, a member of the Red Help Organization (RHO) in the Netherlands. She was recruited by the PFLP to do a casing of the Lod airport in Israel. While on this mission she was arrested. Her psychological assessment confirmed she was 13 years old when she began visiting bars. A few years later she began to drink heavily. About this time she was gang-raped and the experience left a deep, mental scar. Her subsequent ties with men were affected by her inner search for her own feminine identity. She could function as a woman in relationships with men only when the men were not particularly masculine. Her preference was for homosexuals and alcoholics.

The second terrorist example is Ilich Ramirez Sanchez, also known as "Carlos," "Cenon Clarke," and "Glen H. Gebhard." He was one of three sons born to a communist Brazilian attorney who named each of his sons after Vladimir Ilich Lenin; one Vladimir, one Illich and one Lenin. Carlos' father and mother were estranged. He was raised by his mother, who he seems to have worshipped. Carlos used women as tools in terrorist operations, but there is no record that he was intimate with them. In fact, he seemed disinterested in sex but boasted of his exploits. Women are comfortable with him because of his evident asexual attitude. His psychological assessment shows his machoism is a means to repress hidden inner feminine feelings. It is also believed his mental outlook is such that he can be triggered to self-destruction.

The only surviving member of the Japanese Red Army (JRA) commando team which executed the Lod Airport massacre in Tel Aviv was Okamoto Kozo, the third example. He is now imprisoned in Israel and reported to be hopelessly deranged. From the beginning of the operation, he believed that he and other JRA members, Yasuda Yasuyuki and Ukudaira Takashi, would be killed and become stars in the constellation Orion. Those they were to kill would also become stars but of a lesser constellation.

Obviously, it is difficult to understand the minds of people such as Janssen, Carlos and Okamoto. Even more difficult is predicting their actions and behavior. Their remoteness and isolation from society which makes it difficult for police, intelligence and security services to obtain information on terrorist activities. The only way in which intelligence can be obtained is through the recruitment of a penetration agent of similar mentality—an improbable happening—or through an agent who can pretend to be of their kind. But agents with this skill and inclination are rare indeed.

9

Personal Security

Former Italian Premier Aldo Moro was a methodical man with a fixed routine. For fifteen years he traveled the same route between his home and his office, at the same time each morning, and regular as clockwork stopped at the same church. As a high-ranking government official, he had bodyguards; but they were old, loyal policemen, none of whom had training in security protection. They literally had not fired their weapons for several years.

Fate caught up with Moro on the morning of March 16, 1978. The day started just like every other day. Moro left his house and walked to the street where his car waited for him as it always did. In back of Moro's car was the escort car with bodyguards. Everyone was relaxed and at ease. Moro slid into the back seat and both cars pulled out into the street. Not far ahead, Moro's driver braked to a screeching halt. A small Fiat 128 blocked the road. Another car drove up from behind and blocked the rear. Moro's guards finally recognized it as a Red Brigade trap, but too late. On the sidewalk, a group of men dressed in Alitalia Airline uniforms stopped their staged conversations, pulled out automatic weapons, and began to fire. In seconds it was over. The bodyguards were dead. Moro was kidnapped and on his way to a terrorist hideout. Careful planning by the terrorists prevented pursuit. The Red Brigade terrorists slashed the tires of vehicles in the immediate area and cut the phone lines. Those who saw what happened could not communicate, and the city swallowed the terrorists before the police even heard of the kidnapping.

The Chauffeur Problem

The ambush was a good one, but Moro had a chance to get away. His chauffeur could have rammed Moro's heavier, bigger car into the smaller blocking Fiat and easily spun it out of the way, but he did not.

While ramming is a good defensive tactic for escaping a trap, I do not know of one case where a chauffeur rammed his way out of a blockade to save his employer. In every case, the chauffeur stopped the car as ordered by the terrorists. The only successful cases where a victim escaped by ramming out of a blockade were those where the intended victim was driving himself.

The chauffeur obeys the blockade because he knows he is not the terrorist's target. The target is his employer in the back seat. If the chauffeur stops, he believes no harm will come to him, but if he speeds up and rams, he knows the terrorists will shoot. Quickly balancing the pros and cons, the chauffeur stops.

Defensive Driving

There are other reasons why it is best for the intended victim to drive the car in terrorist situations. His mind becomes alert and focused on the scene. The adrenalin flows and the driver becomes the complete defensive driver. A defensive driver performs as follows:

1. The driver is observant and vigilant. His eyes are on the road and the area ahead looking for anything out of the ordinary. If something appears suspicious, he tries to avoid it. He backs up, finds another street, or goes around the block and selects a new route. He is familiar with the area and he knows the streets.

2. The driver will drive as far to the left as possible because an overtaking terrorist will pass on the left to force the victim's car to the right.

3. If the driver takes along another person for protection, he should use the "buddy system."

This requires prior planning because without planning two men, not one, are in danger. There is no point in taking an unarmed person along for protection. What good is he? He must be armed. He should not sit in the front seat next to the driver, because in countries with left hand drive danger generally comes from the left, and the buddy cannot shoot to the left without firing across the face of the driver. The buddy must sit in the back seat, leaning forward, looking in all directions for trouble with his gun ready. If trouble comes from the left the buddy can easily handle it from the rear seat. If it comes from the left front, the buddy leans forward, arms extended past the driver's face and fires. He does not interfere with or harm the driver.

On reaching the destination, the buddy does not remain in the car where he would be a sitting duck to a sidewalk assailant. Nor does he accompany the driver into his meeting, which might be an ambush. Instead the buddy leaves the car and takes a position, as inconspicuously as possible, near a tree, a doorway, even a lamp post, and alertly watches the area with his weapon ready. If trouble comes, he shoots from his place of protection. The noise will probably force the terrorists to leave as quickly as they can.

One lesson learned from past vehicle ambush cases is that the guard's weight rests *against* his pistol, making a swift drawn impossible. This led to several changes in the use of the pistol holster. When approaching a danger area the pistol should be drawn and placed under the thigh. If loose on the seat, sudden braking or ramming will propel the gun to the floor, out of reach. Some police officers have designed special holsters attached to the front seat of their patrol cars. In dangerous situations the pistol is placed in the holster which hangs between the policeman's legs, easily in reach.

The defensive driver's checklist continues:

4. Vehicles are driven with doors locked and windows raised.

5. Seat belts are fastened. If not, the driver when ramming would hit his head on the windshield.

6. Armor plate protects the driver if he rams the blockade.

A simple, effective armor consists of one half-inch thick aluminum plate. It protects against handguns and machineguns, is inexpensive, lightweight, and needs no maintenance. My suggestion is that it is needed only for protection from the rear because after breaking through a blockade, it is only the rear end of the vehicle which is exposed to terrorist gunfire. Armor plate can be installed quickly on the back of the front and rear seats. Ordinarily this is adequate protection, but where the terrorists' modus operandi is to throw hand grenades under moving cars, sheets of armor plate can be installed under the floorboards of the car.

7. Vehicles are parked by the defensive driver in protected places, not overnight in the street. Parked cars are always locked.

8. The defensive driver inspects his car for any noticeable wires which might indicate the car has been rigged with explosives. If wires are seen, call the police. Do not try to deal with this situation yourself.

The Haig Incident

On June 25, 1979 an unsuccessful attempt was made to assassinate General Alexander Haig, the NATO commander, near Mons, Belgium. This incident provided a useful example for students of personal security. As Haig's chauffeur-driven Mercedes passed over a small bridge during his morning commute to Supreme Headquarters, a large explosive charge blew up in the road just behind it. The explosion caused only minor damage to Haig's car, but left a ten foot crater and hurled basketball-sized chunks of pavement through the windshield of the trailing security vehicle, slightly injuring three bodyguards. Afterwards, police investigators found a detonator wire 500 feet long, as well as a walkie-talkie and a construction worker's hat.

A little more than week after the attack, a newspaper in Charleroi, Belgium, received a letter from the Andreas Baader Commandos, Red Army Faction, claiming responsibility for the attack. The letter contained extremely precise details of the attack and explained in the terrorists' opinion why the attempt failed. They wrote that they made a technical error; the general's car was traveling at a speed of 2 meters per tenth of a second, which was the time it required to manually detonate the 20 kilograms of explosives contained in the charge. As a result, the explosion occurred right between the general's car and that of the escort following it. Obviously, the terrorists had triggered the charge at the moment Haig's car passed over it instead of allowing lead time to compensate for the car's speed.

The attempt against Haig is a landmark case. Although Haig varied his route to NATO headquarters, the attack against him was made on his alternate route. It is the only known case where this has been done. What can be learned from the case is that Haig was considered an important enough target to warrant additional risk.

The terrorists certainly surveilled Haig many times to discover both his main route and the alternate one. Upon seeing the alternate route's small bridge and adjacent terrain, the terrorists concluded that it was the best place to ambush Haig's heavily protected limousine. The site was well suited for an attack by bombing—the tactic used in roughly 70 percent of all terrorist acts—eliminating the necessity to confront the bodyguards face-to-face.

Residence Security

The security of a residence is of considerable importance. Residences are often the targets of internal terrorists as in the case of the Chandler assassination in Sao Paulo, the murder of Ponto in Frankfurt, and others in Teheran. The residence, however, is not the most desirable target because it *can* be protected. The terrorist prefers to attack his victim on the street, but when the terrorist finds that the victim is not a person of fixed routine, he must look elsewhere for a suitable ambush site. He can move the ambush site closer to the victim's place of employment. But this is risky because it will generally be located in the downtown area where there is too great a possibility of police presence. The ambush-minded terrorist prefers the quieter residential areas and will check the victim's neighborhood. If the terrorist sees that the victim's home is protected, he might decide on a different target.

Residential security is not difficult when viewed as a military defense zone. The first defense is the outer perimeter. The following are several suggestions on how to build the outer defense:

1. In most foreign countries homes are surrounded by walls or fences; if not, erect a high fence. Top the wall or fence with barbed wire. Make it difficult to scale.
2. Gates are locked. If the terrorist enters he must climb over the perimeter fence or wall.
3. Trip wires can easily be installed on top of the fence or on the ground to set off an alarm when tripped.
4. Install an outdoor, perimeter lighting system.
5. Remove shielding shrubbery which could conceal terrorist movement.
6. Guards and dogs should be posted in the perimeter area. Do not become friendly with the guards. Instead, keep

them on the alert. The guard should be as alert to your frequent spot checks of him as he is of terrorists.

The next control zone of security includes points of entry into the residence. Most entry controls are the use of common sense and equipment:

1. Install iron bars or a grill over windows.
2. Prevent entry through openings for air conditioners or pipes by installing iron bars.
3. Mount a wide-range viewer in the door.

There are several differences in the modus operandi of a burglar and a terrorist. Homes are burglarized when the residents are absent. Terrorists hit the residence when they know the victim is present. To defend against this tactic, family members and domestic help must be instructed not to give out information on the telephone. They should not reveal who is or is not at home or when they are expected.

During the Dominican Revolution another officer and I lodged for the night in a private home requisitioned by the American Embassy. It was empty except for several canvas cots, and was located on the edge of no man's land, with the rebel lines a block away. The caretaker was an elderly Dominican. At one o'clock in the morning, the phone rang and we awoke to hear the one-sided conversation of the caretaker in Spanish:

"Hello. Yes this is 321 Molina Street . . . Yes, the third house from the corner of Bolivar . . . You're right. The American Embassy is renting the house. . . . Yes there are Americans . . . Yes . . .Yes . . . There are only two of them . . . Goodnight."

The other officer and I quickly gathered our clothes, left by the back door and made our way to the Embassy where we spent the rest of the night.

Draperies in residences should be drawn. It keeps burglars guessing whether anyone is at home and it confuses terrorists as to whether the victim is present

Employee Security

The more difficult part of protecting the residence against penetration by terrorists depends on the human factor. It is very difficult to obtain complete security and loyalty from domestic servants; it is asking too much to expect it. I know of numerous cases where domestic services gave information on their employers to terrorists. I *cannot* recall a single case where a servant warned his employer of a possible terrorist operation against the employer. It is not difficult to understand why. The servant is part of the local community and is subject to pressures by family and friends who belong to, or are sympathizers of, an internal terrorist group. It is difficult to resist pressure by friends and family. The foreign employer is only temporary. He stays only a short time and the servant is again left with family and friends.

There are two rules which apply to the security relationship with domestic servants and employees:

1. Do not expect an employee to be responsible for the security of an employer.
2. Maintain a strict employer-employee relationship.

Do not confide in your servants. Do not try to make them a member of your family. Brief them on the security practices they must follow with the understanding that if they do not they will be fired. If they become lax in security, terminate their employment. The others will then learn. But do not expect that domestic servants will remember your instructions. They must be repeated regularly.

The high points for briefing domestic help are:

1. Identity every caller before opening the door.
2. Do not allow any unknown person into the house.
3. Never accept a package unless it is expected.
4. Never tell anybody who is at home, or when someone is expected.
5. Report anything suspicious.

If a servant knows that the employer is security conscious it helps the employee turn down requests for information on the employer from relatives and friends. There are many people who do not practice security so there is little reason for terrorists to select one who does.

Personal Security

The last line of defense is the personal security of the intended victim. It is also the most demanding and difficult defense because self-enforced discipline is needed. It is tiring, and mistakes take place, routine sets in and vulnerabilities occur. People who live in terrorist environments and practice security need to rest and relax occasionally in a peaceful non-terrorist environment. Afterwards, they can return and deal with the rigors of living with terrorism.

Never be ashamed or embarrassed of being security-conscious. Personal security is a serious business. Never take it lightly. Never let terrorists assume you are lax. If you do it shows them that you are an ideal target.

The next two chapters analyze specific techniques of personal security in detail.

10
How to Ram

Defensive driving, such as ramming a vehicle through a terrorist roadblock, is a means by which to escape from a terrorist trap. I know several people who have rammed not only out of terrorist traps but out of roadblocks set up by bandits, guerrilla forces, and even the police. However, ramming must be kept in perspective. It is a last resort, a drastic means of escape. Ramming must be preceded by a constant exercise of personal security, and a continuing sensitivity toward any suspicious activity which would indicate that a terrorist act is in the offing.

A common terrorist tactic is to intercept their victim while he is in his automobile. Even this blockade can be broken by the determined driver who has planned ahead. The first requirement is a car which has enough power for the job. For this purpose a medium-powered American car is best. Small, low-powered European and Japanese cars do not have the power nor the weight to push aside a blocking vehicle. Any attempt to ram with a low-powered car may fail, with the ramming vehicle becoming "hung-up" on the blocking car.

Roadblock Operations

As the terrorist undertakes a roadblock operation, he comes under pressure. He knows he has to plan his action thoroughly to avoid being injured, wounded, or captured by the local police. As the succession of roadblock cases in Brazil and elsewhere have shown, the terrorists' modus operandi is as follows:

1. The terrorists will carefully select the ambush site along the victim's known route of travel. It must satisfy two requirements. The site must be one where the victim can be

surprised and overwhelmed. Secondly, the site must offer a good escape route.

2. The terrorists do not want to risk an encounter with the police. They will plan and practice the act of terror until they can execute it within one or two minutes, and then retreat to a place of safety.

The most common tactic used by terrorists to block a street requires parking one or two cars in such a way as to obstruct passage. It is known as a stationary roadblock. If the victim detects the roadblock far enough away from it to reverse his direction, escaping by another route is the best defense. But terrorists try to block the road at a point where the obstruction can be seen only when the victim is immediately upon it. It is then too late to reverse and back the car out of danger.

When a victim first spots the blockade, he will see terrorists standing by the side of the blocking car. Several others may be in the car or possibly on the other side of the blocking car. As the victim brakes his car, the terrorists will start to move toward the victim's car with the intent of pulling him out and taking him hostage.

Although the terrorists appear formidable, they are also vulnerable. They are on open ground, and if the victim's vehicle suddenly lurches forward, the terrorists can either stand their ground, fire at the vehicle, and be run over, or they can run out of the way. To date in every case where ramming has occurred, the terrorists have chosen to run away. Running to safety does give the terrorists the option of firing at the escaping vehicle, but there are problems with this tactic. The terrorist does not want to shoot into any of the blocking cars because in all probability they are also his escape vehicles. Nor does he want to shoot into the other terrorists. By this time the ambush scene is near chaos with no one in the place they were assigned to be, and no clear field of fire.

Ramming

When the victim first sees the blockade ahead of him he should act as the terrorists expect him to. He should begin to slow down. While doing so he should not steer his vehicle onto the side of the road. He must maintain the best road position (toward the center) for the ramming operation. The victim should come to a perceptible stop some ten to fifteen feet from the blocking vehicle. The accelerator must now be fully depressed from the moment the ramming operation begins until it is over. It is the power of the ramming vehicle, not the impact of collision, that will push the blocking vehicle out of the way.

One difficulty in teaching ramming techniques is the abnormality in teaching good, safe drivers to do something they have previously been taught not to do: smashing deliberately into another car. In one case, where a government chauffeur with many years of driving experience was being taught defensive driving, he could not bring himself to ram into another car. He just could not do it and was therefore excused from the class. It had nothing to do with the fear of injury because there is no danger of injury to the driver in ramming. At speeds of even up to thirty miles an hour there is little shock or tendency to lose control of the car. It is mandatory, however, that seat belts be buckled by all of the occupants of the ramming car. And because the terrorists will not be wearing seat belts and may even be getting out of the car at the time of the ramming, it is the terrorists in the blocking car who will receive a tremendous jolt. Generally it is of such force that it will scatter their weapons, making it extremely doubtful that anyone in the blocking car will be able to fire at the fleeing car.

Those terrorists who are not in the blocking vehicle may have the opportunity to fire at the escaping car, as they did in the case of Consul Curtis Cutter. Yet there is not a single recorded case where the terrorists pursued the victim. They have too many other concerns at the time. They must first see to the needs of any injured terrorists who were struck or run over. The struck vehicle is also an escape vehicle and the terrorists must determine if it is still operable. If not, other usable transportation must be located. The primary concern of the terrorists is to escape from the blockade scene before the police arrive.

The ramming vehicle must strike the blocking car with a solid blow. The best method is to steer the car directly at, or shortly behind, the rear wheel of the blocking car. On impact, continue to accelerate. The blocking car will spin around and allow the ramming vehicle to escape. If it is impossible to ram the rear wheel area of the blocking vehicle, the ramming car should be steered to hit the front wheel area.

The car's front is more difficult to move because of the engine weight there. The ramming operation is therefore slightly slower, with the ramming vehicle exposed seconds longer than when ramming the rear wheel zone.

There are a few dos and don'ts of ramming:

1. The ramming vehicle must always hit the blocking vehicle at an angle. The sharper the angle the greater the impact to the occupants of the blocking car; if the angle is slight the ramming vehicle may be able to squeeze through forcibly with little impact. Under no circumstances, however, can the ram be made broadside against the blocking vehicle. In most broadside hits the ramming vehicle becomes entangled with the blocking car, and is forced to halt.
2. Care must be taken to hit the proper impact area. If two cars block the road, try to hit only one car to escape and try to hit it in the rear wheel area.
3. Injure as many terrorists as possible. It creates confusion and minimizes the number of terrorists who might be able to fire at the escaping car. If one of the two blocking vehicles contains a greater number of terrorists, ram into it and stun and injure as many as you can.

The most vulnerable area of the ramming vehicle is in the front end, primarily because of the radiator. On impact the radiator might be forced back into the fan, puncturing it and releasing the car's coolant. It makes little difference. Keep driving. Even with no water in the radiator a car can travel for four to five miles, well beyond the reach of the terrorists.

Here is a helpful hint for those living in areas of regular terrorist activity. Reinforce your vehicle's front bumper by welding a two inch pipe to the car frame immediately in back of the front bumper. The pipe is out of sight and for all appearances the car is unchanged. It is, however, a sturdy ramming accessory protecting the radiator as well.

Lastly, keep the car doors locked at all times. It will help keep the doors from popping open on impact.

11

Firearms: The Last Defense

When the armed victim is trapped by terrorists and cannot run away, his weapon represents his only hope; his last chance. Consequently, the victim must understand how to properly use his weapon before going overseas. The first U.S. government-sponsored courses in weaponry were created to give firearm instruction to people going overseas into terror-plagued areas. Most trainees had never carried a gun before, and the great majority were reluctant to do so. Americans believed that to carry a gun was uncivilized, and perhaps rightly so, but terrorism itself is something apart from civilization. Because of this reluctance many private protection firms do not offer firearms training to the American business executives they advise. However, I believe that if a defense exists, it must be understood and used as a defensive option.

A number of psychological problems were uncovered while teaching weaponry to people who had never handled a gun. Trainees questioned their own ability to simply fire a weapon, even at an assailant who was trying to kill them. They doubted their own ability to respond. They doubted that they could raise a gun and fire it at a terrorist. To overcome these doubts, they were told that they would react as they were trained to react because training would bring an automatic response. When the terrorist came after them they would see him as another silhouette target popping up and they would fire, automatically, at the target. Some trainees accepting this advice rationalized that when they fired, they would shoot only to wound. Yet, this response inevitably leads to the death of the fair-minded trainee.

A gunfight is not a sporting event and it allows no room for fair play. In a terrorist gunfight the enemy is out to kill and the victim's only defense is to kill him first.

It is preferable to run away from a gunfight because it is difficult to hit a running man with a handgun. Statistics for the U.S. show that the average distance between police and criminals in gunfights is twelve feet or less. This may seem a very short distance, but if a victim is twelve feet or more away from an armed terrorist, escape by running is a good defensive move.

Whether the intended kidnap victim should use a gun depends on what kind of situation he is in. If in the past the victim was released by the terrorists, then the intended victim should not resist but take his chances. However, if the situation occurs in an advanced state of internal terrorism, where the victim will likely be murdered, the intended victim should try to resist or run away.

The objective in a gunfight with terrorists is to put each terrorist out of action as quickly as possible, preferably with one shot into each. It is not a situation which compares with a policeman dealing with a thief or petty criminal. The terrorist situation is one of warfare where the enemy is out to kill. The terrorist outnumbers and outguns the victim. The victim must deal with multiple, moving targets. The victim must hit each terrorist quickly, then move on to the others. The victim will always face an attack where he must engage more than one terrorist. Terrorists are never so fairminded as to give the victim a one-on-one encounter.

In any event, the victim should keep moving because a moving target is harder to hit. The victim should move toward any kind of cover he can find whether it is a tree, a wall, or even a curb. The victim can fall to the ground and roll toward cover. A rolling target is small and difficult to hit. But in moving toward cover, it is recommended that the victim move to the left rather than to the right, if possible. The majority of assailants are right-handed, and as a result have a tendency to shoot to their left. In the gripping of a pistol, an extra-right or nervous grip will turn the weapon in that direction.

Frontier Lessons

When compiling basic research on the reactions of a gunfighter, there were few places to find information. Eventually the search led to the early American frontier and the sheriffs, the Texas Rangers, and the marshalls who tamed the West. One Texas Ranger said, "If you get in a gunflight, don't let yourself feel rushed. Take your time fast."

Most frontier lawmen agreed that during the initial confusion of a gunfight the first bullets generally miss their targets. As the bullets fly the gun fighter should resolve to himself that he is going to put a bullet into his adversary. It should be his fixation, his motivating force to sustain him during the battle.

One of the most famous lawmen, Wyatt Earp, reputedly never fired the first shot. Calmly, as he was shot at, Earp took careful aim and killed his opponent.

Other advice passed down from the American frontier was to have courage and keep shooting at the assailant as long as possible, even if wounded. Many badly wounded men have killed their adversaries, and many dying men have killed their killers. To this day, the rule is to keep shooting until it is no longer humanly possible.

Firearm Selection

In terrorist situations the intended victim should arm himself with the biggest, heaviest gun he can handle. He needs a big, booming firearm, which will not only show the terrorist he means business, but will fire a bullet through doors, cars, break bones, and disable an enemy with one shot. A .22 caliber or similar small size caliber weapon is not only inappropriate, but also adds risk to the victim. The .22 round is simply not big enough to reliably stop a human target unless an extremely vital organ is hit. If counter-attacked with a .22, the terrorists will immediately realize that the victim is using a small caliber gun, indicating that he is either inexperienced or unprepared. The terrorists will move in for the kill. However, when he hears loud return fire from the victim's firearm, he will likely conclude he is up against a trained adversary. Even though he may not immediately leave, it is more than enough to dissuade him from charging the victim.

The best counterterrorist weapon is the shotgun. It was the ten gauge shotgun, not the revolver, which won the American West. It is a powerful weapon. Aiming is secondary and its effect devastating. Unfortunately it is big. It cannot be easily carried in the streets or office building. Therefore, the shotgun is best used as a defensive weapon in the residence and place of employment. A handgun is carried for protection in the street and along the route of travel from residence to office.

The .45 caliber automatic and the 9 mm Browning automatic, both heavy service pistols, are recommended as counterterrorist handguns. The automatic is recommended over the revolver for several reasons:

1. The automatic is more reliable than the revolver. It can be easily taken apart and repaired while the revolver, on the other hand, is a precision instrument as fine as a watch. If a mechnical difficulty develops it must be sent to a gunsmith.

2. An automatic fed by an ammunition clip is far easier to reload, particularly in the middle of a gunfight, than a revolver which requires that each bullet be individually inserted in the chamber. When a clip is empty, it is released and falls out. A full clip is slapped in within two seconds. In contrast, the intended victim who uses a revolver must carry his extra ammunition loose in his pocket. In a terrorist situation, as he runs and rolls on the ground, there is the possibility that bullets will be lost. When he reloads, the revolver must be broken open, the shells ejected and the chamber reloaded. The terrorist will take advantage of the reloading time to close in.

3. An automatic fires at four or five times the rate of a revolver and provides the intended victim with a substantial amount of firepower. Because of this firepower the automatic is more effective in combatting nighttime ambushes. Terrorists prefer night operations. Carlos Marighella wrote, "Night assault is usually the most advantageous to the urban terrorist. It is ideal for surprise, it facilitates flight and hides the identity." A tactic to defend against nighttime assault is called "alley-cleaning." When the intended victim sees the muzzle blast of the terrorist's gun, he fires a burst slightly to the right of where he saw the blast. It should hit the terrorist. A revolver, however, cannot fire fast enough for effective "alley-cleaning."

4. A number of police departments have changed from the .38 caliber revolver to the .45 automatic. One reason is

hitting power. In nineteen of twenty-two cases in one study of the .45's effectiveness, the criminal was killed with one shot. In the remaining cases, although the criminal was not killed with one shot, he was put out of action.

The Point Method

Because the intended victim of a terrorist ambush will be faced with multiple, moving targets, the conventional method of firing a handgun has been replaced with the faster point method of shooting. The point method is based upon the fact that people have an inner-sensing ability to point their index finger accurately at any target. That target may be to the left or right of the victim or even behind out of his range of vision. The point system is based entirely upon teaching the trainee to imagine that his index finger is the barrel of his handgun. First, the trainee must learn how the correct grip feels. He practices until he can automatically assume the proper grip so that the gun barrel simulates his index finger. Using the point method, it takes only a short time to make a good marksman out of someone who has never before fired a weapon.

The point system of shooting is well suited to confrontations with terrorists because there is little time to aim a handgun carefully before shooting at terrorists. Also with the point system, it is possible to fire quite accurately even though the victim is simultaneously running and shooting to give himself covering fire. However, there are times when the point system should give way to carefully aimed single shots to kill the assailant. This happens when the victim has reached cover and the terrorist approaches across an open space intent upon reaching and killing the victim. When this situation takes place, the victim should carefully aim his weapon with both hands and fire a bullet into a vital area of the approaching terrorist.

The most vulnerable areas of the human body to gunshot wounds are the head, chest, and long bones. Easiest to hit is the stomach area in the middle of the body. Here the bullet will do maximum damage. There are big bones in the pelvic area, and when the bullet enters and breaks bones the terrorist will be out of action. A bullet in the intestines will send a terrorist into paralyzing hydrostatic shock.

Terrorist Vulnerabilities

In almost all cases the terrorist's intended victim believes he does not have the slightest chance of successfully resisting the terrorists by shooting back at them. He believes that there is no defense against their greater manpower and firepower. This is not true. Terrorists have their vulnerabilities. To begin with, time is on the side of the victim. Terrorists surveil the victim and case the ambush site so they can execute the terrorist act in one minute or less. Terrorists want everything their own way. Their best chance for survival is to execute the kidnapping or murder and leave the area as quickly as possible. It is doubtful that terrorists will stay in the action site for more than two minutes. It can safely be assumed that three minutes would be an inordinate amount of time for a terrorist to stay at the ambush scene. That being the case, the intended victim's sole mission in a gunfight with terrorists is to keep them at bay for no more than three minutes.

A terrorist has a great fear of being wounded. He knows that if he is wounded, he will fall and be abandoned by his cohorts and become a police prisoner. In most countries he will endure harsh interrogation before he receives medical treatment. He will reveal everything, and when he has finished he is of no further value to the police nor to the terrorists. His life is in jeopardy. Knowing this, when he sees and hears the ambushed victim responding with gunfire, it adds a risk that he fears greatly. The chances are good that he will retreat.

The Decision to Arm

There still remain a number of people who will refuse to carry a gun under any circumstance. In fact, they will even refuse instruction in weaponry. This is a bad decision in terrorist situations. For example, there is the case where nine terrorists belonging to the People's Revolutionary Army (ERP) broke into the home of the director of the United States Information Agency in Cordoba, Argentina. Armed with pistols and automatic weapons, their mission was to kidnap the American. But somehow the surprised victim quickly recovered, wrestled a pistol from a terrorist, and held his would-be abductors at gunpoint. He pointed the pistol at the terrorists until they noticed he did not know how to release the safety catch on the gun. Without the slightest danger to himself, a terrorist deliberately drew his own pistol and shot the American in the lower abdomen, knocking him to the floor. The terrorists vented their rage and pistol-whipped him, administered drugs, and dragged him off to their car.

Sadly enough, a minimal amount of firearm instruction would have prevented this abduction.

12

Responding To Terrorism

"It's 10:00 o'clock on a Saturday morning. A security officer, on morning duty, is alone catching up on paperwork of the past week. The telephone rings and as he answers it, a voice screams out, 'Help! For God's sake help! They've taken over the central clinic, about five men wearing hoods. My God, they've got a hundred people in here!' Click. The phone is dead."

With this scenario I open my lectures to foreign security officials to demonstrate why it is so necessary to prepare for a terrorist situation. Terrorism occurs unexpectedly, without warning, usually at night or during a holiday. If the security forces have not planned in advance to effectively deal with the situation, it is difficult for them to do so spontaneously. However, only a few countries have formulated plans to respond to a terrorist act. Because of this, most countries have blundered along, consequently sustaining a loss of life. The United States is no exception.

A tragic incident occurred during the terrorists' seizure of the Saudi Arabian Embassy in Khartoum. It resulted in the murder of United States Ambassador Noel, Deputy Chief of Mission Moore, and the Belgian Charge d'Afaires, Eid. On March 1, 1973 a Black September Organization hit team seized the Saudi Arabian Embassy during an afternoon social gathering of the diplomatic community. The terrorists' objective was to obtain the release of seventeen prisoners, including Sirhan Sirhan and Abu Daud, who had planned and executed the Munich Olympic massacre. When Washington was informed of the incident a task force was convened immediately with a Department of State official of undersecretary rank in charge. The task force was alarmed that the Embassy in Khartoum was without an ambassador, and it was felt that the best possible leadership should be at the scene of the action. The undersecretary left for Khartoum to take command.

While the Washington task force waited for the arrival of their chief in Khartoum, the urgency of the undersecretary's flight was unexplainably ignored. He was bumped from a U.S. Air Force jet and found himself crossing the Atlantic in a slower plane. Time was crucial, and the situation was made worse when a sandstorm closed the Khartoum airport, forcing the undersecretary to return to Cairo. It was only after the murder of Noel, Moore, and Eid that the undersecretary deplaned in Khartoum.

A valuable lesson was learned from the Khartoum murders. The head of a task force is in charge and must stay in the command center on top of the situation, because he has the responsibility for making decisions. Had the United States government been prepared for such an incident, it is doubtful that the undersecretary would have left his command. However, mistakes happen frequently in the handling of terrorist incidents. I shall make a number of suggestions to correct errors made in earlier terrorists situations

Fighting Terrorism

My first suggestion for counterterrorists is that they plan ahead to be in readiness with manpower, equipment and finances. In other words, prior planning is vital.

The massacre of the Israeli Olympic team in Munich by the Black September Organization (BSO) points out the need for prior planning. It was early morning, long before dawn, on September 5, 1972 when eight BSO terrorists, seven men and one woman, surreptitiously penetrated the darkness of the Olympic Village. Using a casing report, they made their way to the living quarters of the Israeli team. They paused, readied themselves, and firing their weapons, broke in on the sleeping athletes. Two Israelis were killed and nine others were taken hostage.

After twenty hours of arduous negotiations, the West German government agreed to permit the terrorists to leave Germany with their hostages. The terrorists demanded air transportation, specifically helicopters, to take them from the Olympic Village to the Fuerstenfeldbruck military airfield for transfer to an international airliner. Hours later an ambush by the German police at the airfield ended in the death of all the hostages, five terrorists, and one German. Three terrorists were captured and jailed. Ali Hassan Salmech had been the BSO planning chief of the operation.

The terrorists did not stay jailed for long. In the following month, on October 29th, two BSO terrorist hijacked a Lufthansa 727 out of Beirut and threatened to blow up the plane unless the three BSO terrorists captured at Munich were released. The Germans agreed. The post-incident investigation of the Munich massacre showed:

1. Before the attack the West German authorities received intelligence reports indicating that a terrorist attack was to be committed in West Germany during the Olympics. Unexplainably, this report was not passed to the security units in Olympic Village. Partially as a result of not having been put on an alert, the security in the Olympic Village was lax.

2. At the Fuerstenfeldbruck ambush site, the police employed five snipers to ambush eight terrorists. It was too few, not even a one-on-one ratio to handle multiple, moving targets. Lives of hostages were at stake and overwhelming firepower was needed. In ambush situations, plan on too much firepower, not too little.

3. The Germans hoped to stage the Fuerstenfeldbruck ambush earlier in the day, and the policy originally planned to transport the terrorists to the airfield by bus. But unexpectedly, the terrorists demanded helicopters and there was a long delay in locating aircraft and a crew. It was dark when the terrorists finally arrived at the airfield. What had been planned as a daytime ambush became a nighttime operation. Everything went wrong. There were too few troops. It was too dark. The snipers tried to shoot terrorists moving through darkness. One terrorist threw a grenade into the hostages and killed them.

A number of lessons were learned from this incident:

1. There is a high risk in trying to rescue hostages from terrorists. A rescue operation must be carefully planned. When a major change takes place, such as in Munich, the entire plan must be revised and revaluated. The change may

be so serious and the risks so great that it is best that the rescue attempt be abandoned.

2. The rescue team must have overwhelming firepower.

International Lessons

As the West German police learned how to best employ a sniper force, so did the Hong Kong police. A high intensity riot broke out in Hong Kong and the sniper force was summoned. It was after hours and the men were called from their homes and told to report at the riot scene. In advance of their arrival the police transported rifles to the area and distributed the weapons. One sharpshooter refused to accept a rifle that he was unfamiliar with. He argued that he did not know how the rifle handled, what the correct sight settings were, and in trying to use it he might kill an innocent person. The police accepted his logic and from that time on the procedure was changed. Each sniper kept possession of his weapon which was zeroed-in and adjusted by the man who would use it.

Two years after Munich, on January 31, 1974 four terrorists belonging to the Popular Front for the Liberation of Palestine (PFLP) and the Japanese Red Army tried to blow up an oil storage tank on Pulau Bukum Island off the coast of Singapore. The attack failed because the terrorist mistook a red-colored storage tank as combustible, which it was not. After the explosion the tank failed to ignite. The terrorists fled and commandeered a ferryboat, the Laju, seizing its five crew members as hostages. They then tried to escape to international waters. A Singaporean gunboat then blocked their way. Complicated negotiations between the terrorists and Singaporean government officials began. The terrorists did not have the leverage they needed. To get the terrorists out of their predicament aboard the Laju, the PFLP executed a back-up operation. They seized the Japanese Embassy in Kuwait and took sixteen hostages. They demanded that the Japanese government fly the four terrorists on the Laju from Singapore to Kuwait and then to a place of refuge. Japan agreed.

The Singaporeans agreed to the demand on condition that the crew be released with Singaporean officials taking their place. The terrorists agreed. The terrorists turned over their weapons when they were aboard the airliner. As an additional precaution to protect the government hostages, the Singaporean security officials meticulously inspected the aircraft and removed everything which the terrorists could use as a weapon, including the flatwear, which was replaced with plastic knives and forks. It seemed a well-planned operation, which it was; even the seating arrangements were planned in advance. However, one Singaporean who was onboard as a hostage explained to me, "I was very nervous, and it was worse when we started to land in Kuwait. I saw troops lining the runway and I didn't know if they were there to welcome us or kill us. I got a sick feeling when I realized we had forgotten to inform the Kuwaitis that we were aboard as hostages. I feared they might think we were all terrorists." On deplaning the same official had difficulty convincing the Kuwaitis that he and the other hostages were Singaporean officials, not terrorists. The Singaporeans had become so involved in the management of the incident that they forgot the protocol of foreign diplomacy.

The Command Center

My next suggestion requires the organization of a command center before terrorists strike. Again, it is a matter of advance planning. Unfortunately, few countries have done so. Among those who have are Singapore, Australia, and Brazil. Other countries, including the United States, seem to believe that an act of terrorism cannot happen to them. It is to their advantage to establish a command center now. In countries where a command center is organized, its members learn how to work together.

The first consideration in organizing a command center is to decide what expertise is needed and to appoint personnel to provide it. It is necessary to select a chief of the command center who will be in charge of the government's response. He should possess intelligence and good judgment and, ideally, a knowledge of police procedure and terror tactics. He should not be a political appointee with few other qualifications. The odds are that a terrorist incident is more likely to turn out badly than well. Unfortunately, this fact is not common enough knowledge to deter political appointees.

The United States' stand on human rights demands that those who are responsible for a terrorist response take extraordinary care in dealing with terrorists, even though the terrorists might have killed or kidnapped an American citizen. When the United States government learns the names and location of the terrorist criminals, it prefers not to pass this information to the local police, fearing a possible violation of the terrorists' human rights. Nor will the United States turn over any information on a terrorist suspect if that information might lead to a violation of his human rights. An official who does so is liable to be federally prosecuted. At minimum, he will be reprimanded, a detriment to his career.

When working with a foreign government's inexperienced security service to free an American hostage, it is important to stay in the background, and not assume any responsibility for the final outcome of the hostage negotiations. Suppose an American citizen is kidnapped in a country that agrees with the United States' concept of human rights, such as Great Britain. The United States government will lend its resources and expertise to help free the hostage. Practically speaking, however, countries such as Great Britain have no need for assistance and will ask for none. On the other hand, underdeveloped countries lack expertise and request help but do not receive it because they may violate the United States' concept of human rights.

I once discussed the problem of selecting the right personnel for a command center with a psychiatrist who has experience in barricade-hostage situations. One of the best negotiators he knew worked during the JRA seizure of the American Embassy in Kuala Lumpur on August 4, 1975. Shortly before noon of that date, five JRA terrorists seized the embassy, taking fifty-three people hostage. As ransom the terrorists demanded that the Japanese government release seven JRA members held in Japanese prisons and fly them to Kuala Lumpur. It presented a difficult situation. American hostages were being held while a third country, Japan, circumvented its own laws by releasing prisoners convicted and sentenced in accordance with Japanese law. Throughout the difficult negotiations the psychiatrist noted that an American embassy officer did an excellent job in dealing with the terrorists. The officer had been an insurance salesman before joining the foreign service and thought his experience as a salesman helped him during the incident. He found many similarities between being a salesman and a go-between with terrorists. The psychiatrist said that good salesmen make good negotiators in terrorist situations. He explained that good salesmen have an intuitive telepathy that registers non-verbal clues expressed by the people they are selling to. Without even knowing it, the salesman's mind adjusts to the person with whom he is dealing and temporarily abandons his own values, adopting those of the person with whom he is dealing. An illusion of comradeship develops.

In addition to police and security officials, other members of the command center might be:

1. A representative of the ranking elected official of the host country.
2. A press officer.
3. A fireman.
4. Officers who have contact in such fields as medical services, transportation, and banking.

Past hostage negotiations with terrorists indicate several other considerations that the command center must plan for. One is the need to locate an aircraft and crew willing to fly terrorists/hostages to diverse destinations, possibly at great risk. Such arrangements must be attainable on a moment's notice—another great difficulty. The other consideration involves ransom funds. When a terrorist kidnapping occurs, the terrorists may demand prompt payment of a large cash sum in exchange for the hostage(s). Again, the command center must be able to fulfill this demand quickly.

I also suggest that as augmenting troops arrive at the area under barricade, a chain of command must be established for all of the units on duty in the area. The units must maintain their operational and personnel structure so they can respond to command.

A case illustrating the basis for this suggestion occurred during the Detroit riots of 1967. The riots were high intensity racial riots involving terrorism. They were of such size and intensity that the local police force could not control the situation. The army was called in. As quickly as the troops arrived they were dispersed all over the city in haphazard fashion. Some were sent to guard buildings, some to hospitals, others to motor pools. Two soldiers were assigned to each fire truck because firefighters were attracting sniper fire.

Later the dispersed troops were needed as a combat force. It was difficult, however, to bring them together as a unit because they had lost their organizational command structure. They were stationed throughout Detroit without their officers or communication gear. Still later when the troops advanced into the riot area, the police mistook them as a hostile force and fired at them. The troops responded and fired back at the police, thinking that they were hostile. Those officers on both sides who knew what was happening could not stop it because the police and the army did not have a common emergency radio channel.

The lessons learned from the Detroit riots apply to terrorist hostage-barricade situations and the use of troops by the command center:

1. Establish a chain of command for all of the units assigned to the barricade.
2. Provide units which are assigned at a distance from the command center with communication equipment.
3. Assign a common emergency radio frequency to be used by all units.

My next suggestion is that the command center initiate and continue negotiations with the terrorists throughout the situation. Many countries refuse to negotiate with terrorists, but in the United States and Western countries negotiation with hostage-holding terrorists is the accepted procedure. The only goal here is to save the lives of the hostages. The only time force is used against terrorists is when it appears certain that the terrorists will murder the hostages. This occurred when the Dutch rescued hostages from the South Moluccans, the Israelis at Entebbe, and the West Germans at Mogadiscio.

The use of negotiations as a tool in hostage situations is largely based upon what is called the Stockholm Syndrome, which takes its name from the previously mentioned bank robbery incident in Stockholm. Before the bandits could escape, the Stockholm police arrived and barricaded the bandits, bank employees, and customers inside the bank. Barricaded together, the bandits and their hostages soon developed a common bond. The hostile attitude they originally held for each other changed and the hostages and bandits began to identify with each other. In fact, after the incident was over one of the clerks married a bandit who had been her captor. The Stockholm Syndrome, highly regarded by government psychiatrists, implies that the longer the negotiations continue, the greater the possibility that the hostages will not be harmed. The bond between terrorist and hostage will grow and friendships will develop. The possibility of using the Stockholm Syndrome to save lives is more viable in cases involving international terrorists, who hold hostages as a means of escape, rather than with internal terrorists who often kill their captives.

Another concept developed during a hostage negotiation incident is known as the Bangkok solution. On December 28, 1972 the Black September Organization (BSO) seized the Israeli Embassy in Bangkok. Six Israelis were held hostage. The terrorists demanded the release of thirty-six internationally-held prisoners. The terrorists executed the incident on the day of the investiture of Thailand's crown prince. The Thai government insisted that nothing mar the festivities. When informed of their poor timing, the terrorists apologized, and the Bangkok solution evolved. The terrorists promised not to commit any act of violence. The Thai government for its part permitted the terrorists to publicize their demands and their cause. They were then safely flown out of Thailand to a place of refuge.

Another useful procedure entails obtaining at least a partial release of the hostages. The more hostages released, the less risky is the use of force to rescue the remaining hostages. Rarely is it possible to negotiate the release of all of the hostages without giving in to the terrorists' demands. On August 2, 1971 a Braniff airliner out of Mexico City was hijacked by an American, Robert Jackson. He was trying to reach Algeria. The plane was diverted to Lima, Rio de Janeiro, and then Buenos Aires, where Jackson held the crew and passengers hostage. A friend of mine in Buenos Aires negotiated with Jackson. He eventually talked Jackson into releasing one hostage after another, until only Jackson remained on board.

After the release of the hostages, Jackson agreed to face-to-face negotiations if they were conducted on board the plane. My friend walked to the plane filled with apprehension. He knew he would have to say something immediately to put Jackson at ease. The plane had a terrible stench about it. The toilets had overflowed and a mixture of feces, urine, and water sloshed in the aisle. Jackson, with his pistol drawn, faced the negotiator, who then said, "You sure as hell got yourself in a shitty mess; now let's sit down and talk about how we can get you out of it."

Jackson relaxed and agreed to surrender. His only condition was that he surrender to a military general. As the hijacker washed and put on a fresh suit, a jeep drove out to the runway and an Argentine general climbed out. In the predawn rain, the hijacker deplaned, and formally surrendered.

If at all possible, the command center should arrange to separate the hostages from the terrorists. In Entebbe the Israeli rescue team had an advantage because not all of the terrorists were in the same room with the hostages. While it is difficult to effect a change of premises, sometimes it can be done by offering the terrorists another location, perhaps with better communications.

I also suggest that the command center maintain communications with the terrorists throughout the incident. Communications should be centralized so that all of the messages pass through a coordinated central point. In some cases this is easily done by the officer in charge of the command center. In other cases, such as the Schleyer kidnapping in West Germany, hundreds of messages were received every day and a separate organization was created to analyze them.

The command center must plan ahead so that all of the logistical and personnel support needs are available at all times. Equipment should include radios, foghorns, special weapons, auxiliary lighting equipment, generators, and other related items.

Personnel are needed to man the barricades and command center around the clock. During the terrorist crises in Brazil, police officers were on duty for five days and nights. A police force cannot keep such a schedule for long without making mistakes. Mistakes are exactly what the terrorists want, because mistakes discredit the government. In the Netherlands, the security forces rotated on eight hour shifts, which is a more satisfactory arrangement that can be accomplished with forethought.

Non-negotiating Countries

Not all countries will negotiate with terrorists. The Soviet Union and Uruguay flatly refuse to negotiate with terrorists. Instead, when faced with a hostage situation, these nations order the terrorists to surrender or face an all-out police assault. The terrorists will almost certainly be killed in the ensuing police barrage. The hostages are also likely to be killed or wounded in the assault. These countries believe that their policy of non-negotiation deters future terrorist attacks because the terrorists know such attacks will end with either their capture or death. The policymakers in the Soviet Union and Uruguay believe that negotiating with terrorists coddles them and encourages more hostage-taking; in the long run more rather than less people will suffer or die.

A number of mysterious details still surround the February 14, 1979 death of United States Ambassador to Afghanistan, Adolph Dubs. In accordance with official policy, the Soviet-trained and led Afghan police charged the room where Dubs was held hostage. When the smoke cleared, Dubs and two of his three abductors were dead. This attack reflects the modus operandi of Soviet-trained police in dealing with a hostage situation. It was at one time also the accepted police procedure in the United States. Previously a kidnapper in the United States was assured that if the police discovered his hideout, he would be surrounded and forced to surrender or be killed.

During the summer of 1958 I participated in negotiations to release twenty-nine American sailors and marines in Cuba. They were kidnapped while returning to the Guantanamo Navy Base by bus and held hostage by the guerrilla forces of Raul Castro. I returned briefly to the base to inform the commanding admiral of the insulting demands made by Castro for the return of the Americans. He weighed the demands and after deliberation concluded that it would be best for the United States to break off negotiations. He believed the first consideration was for the well-being of his country. As a nation the U.S. had often lost more than twenty-nine men while protecting its security. The admiral believed that the loss of the hostage's lives was acceptable because of this reason.

The incident in Cuba was a forerunner of numerous revolutionary kidnappings that have since plagued the entire world. The unanswered question is whether hostage-taking would have escalated to such worldwide proportions if the United States government would have refused to negotiate with the Cuban terrorists.

Conclusion

In conclusion, the collection of intelligence on terrorists in both internal and international situations is highly recommended. Besides being a useful tool, such intelligence is not as disruptive as other police measures taken to control terrorist actions. In Istanbul terrorists frustrated the police, who placed the city under a twenty-four hour curfew while an army of 80,000 men searched the city, block by block, for terrorists. None were found, but the curfew restricted the movement of hundreds of thousands of people, alienating many who then switched their support to the terrorists.

A better method of obtaining intelligence on terrorists is through "wanted" posters and rewards. Their use was the principal means by which the West German terrorists were brought to justice. The Baader-Meinhoff Gang was decimated through posters and rewards.

A more bizarre use of the reward method occurred in the Dominican Republic. On June 12, 1959 Cuban expeditionaries and Dominican exiles invaded the island in a three-pronged attack. The Dominican Army retreated and their collapse was prevented only by the newly formed Dominican Foreign Legion, which encircled the mountain strongholds of the invading guerrillas. General Trujillo informed the peasants that the government would pay $1,000 reward for each guerrilla head turned in to government authorities. The otherwise apolitical peasants suddenly became hospitable hosts. They invited the guerrillas into their huts, where they wined and dined them. When the terrorists slept, the peasants chopped off their heads. The commander of the legion said that because of this reward offer, the Dominican Republic is not a communist state today.

We cannot turn our backs on terrorism. It will not go away because it has been extremely successful, and an enemy has never given up successful tactics. Through terrorism, a number of governments friendly to the United States have collapsed. Others are near collapse. It is entirely possible that Western governments could be weakened and destroyed from within through the skillful application of terrorist tactics. If this happens, terrorism will prove to have been the single most successful war tactic of this century.

Epilogue

In October 1979, the author delivered a lecture on international terrorist links to a seminar on counterterrorism in Montivideo, Uruguay. The following epilogue is excerpted from his address there.

* * *

"The remarks I make to you today will concern what I call *The Crimson Web of Terror*. This is the term I use to refer to the ever-growing linkages between various international terrorist insurgent groups.

"The true enemy in all cases of terrorist insurgency is international communism, led by the Soviet Union. But many officials, including the present administration in Washington, refuse even to consider possible connections between insurgency in Spain or Iran with the Soviet Union. Why? Because firstly, the Washington administration would have to take action against such a connection. Secondly, confirmation of the connection would influence international political maneuvers such as Salt II. An American motorist waiting in a gas line could hardly be expected to favor Salt II, knowing of the Soviet involvement in Iran's revolution.

"The official policy of the Soviet Union, however, is quite clear: 'The Soviet Union is opposed to acts of terrorism which disrupt the diplomatic activities of States and their representatives, transport communications between them and the normal course of international contacts and meetings. It is quite inadmissable to extend the concept of international terrorism to the national liberation struggle, to actions offering resistance to an aggressor on territories occupied by him and to working people's demonstrations for their rights against oppression by exploiters.'

"This Soviet policy statement is interpreted to mean that publicly the Soviet Union is opposed to terrorist acts which seize embassies and hold diplomats hostage. It means the Soviets are opposed to hijacking, or any other terrorist act that disrupt international meetings. In reality, the Soviets are opposed only to a specific category of terrorist action which they perceive as threatening to countries occupied by Soviet armies. However, the Soviets are not opposed to terrorist acts committed by revolutionary groups, such as the Red Brigades, nor national liberation movements, such as the Basque separatists or the Zimbabwe guerrillas, nor workers organizations, such as the Socialist Workers Party or the Communist Labor Party.

"The command structure by which the Soviets are able to guide, support, train and fund worldwide terrorism and insurgency is through two separate entities. One is State operated. The other is an organization encompassing Cuba and the Palestine Liberation Organization (PLO) as well. Both offer a short, secure link for communications and support.

"Cuba's security agency, the Directorate General of Intelligence (DGI) is largely controlled by a KGB liaison team that shares offices within the DGI headquarters in Havana. By western standards this is highly unusual but it is a common Soviet intelligence practice, also used by them in the Soviet Bloc countries to effectively control another country's intelligence service. It provides the optimum method of communication and a secure channel to provide support ranging from advice and finance to equipment and weaponry. A special fund is supplied by the KGB to the DGI to enable the DGI to carry out foreign missions on its behalf. Although the exact size of the subsidy is not known, the extent of it becomes apparent upon analysis. The DGI, for example, has as its main target the United States, yet it also has six other divisions to spy on the rest of the world. The DGI also sponsors other non-geographical divisions, such as the "Illegals," who are both operational as well as supportive of the other seven divisions. By no stretch of the imagination can it be believed that the Cuban intelligence and subversion operations are funded by Cuba alone. Furthermore, the DGI and Cuba provide support for various national liberation movements which in Africa alone represents more than 50,000 Cuban military and insurgency advisers. There is no doubt that the Cuban intelligence and insurgency efforts, measured in personnel stationed abroad, dwarfs the U.S. intelligence and counterinsurgency efforts against it.

"Aside from the surrogate role of Cuba, its importance to the Soviet Union cannot be minimized. For instance, following the 1962 Missile Crisis, Premier Nikita Khrushchev was attacked verbally in the Supreme Soviet for withdrawing missiles from Cuba. He pointed a finger at his accuser and asked, "Does not a socialist state remain in the Caribbean, protected by the United States itself?" Seven years later to the month, the Soviet Brigade crisis arose in Cuba, with the Soviets and Cubans explaining that it was a training unit, nothing more. An analysis revealed, however, that the brigade was an elite guard to protect the electronic and communication intelligence installations the Soviets constructed in Cuba to monitor the continental U.S.

"It is much the same with the PLO. Their primary contact point is Beirut. There Yasir Arafat, the PLO chieftain, is in daily contact with Soviet Ambassador Aleksandar Soldatov. Funds are provided through direct contact in Beirut and Moscow via religious front groups and bank transfers in Switzerland and elsewhere. Most PLO logistical supplies are furnished by the Soviets through overt arms shipments by way of Lebanon and various training camps in Yemen and elsewhere. Other logistical help, including weaponry, is provided by the Soviets through governmental cutouts such as Libya.

"From these foci of terrorism and insurgency emanate the contacts and linkage for worldwide terrorist groups. These centers provide small, indigenous revolutionary groups with the advice, guidance and support necessary to promote insurgency against non-communist governments who are allied with the U.S.

"The best place to begin an examination of this crimson web of terror is in West Germany because from its geographical position alone it ties the East with the West. Furthermore, two generations of terrorists were destroyed in West Germany and the ashes of destruction can be sifted for evidence. Lastly, there are defections of German terrorists and their revelations have proved invaluable in piecing together international connections between terrorist leaders and organizations.

"In 1968 Andreas Baader and his girlfriend fled Frankfurt, Germany to escape sentencing by a German court for his previous arson conviction. They went to Paris and stayed in the vacant apartment of Regis Debray. Debray was cooling his heels in a Bolivian jail at the time for his participation in the ill-fated expedition of Che Guevara. Baader's housing was arranged between Debray's father, a lawyer, and Baader's legal counsel, Siegfried Haag, who was also a terrorist leader. Through this housing arrangement we immediately have evidence of ties between incipient German terrorism and Cuba, Che Guevara and Regis Debray. Baader and his girlfriend then received money and airline tickets to Bogota, Colombia—being among the first to travel the Paris-to-Bogota terrorist highway. From Bogota they traveled to Italy, Switzerland and then on to West Berlin to meet with Ulrike Meinhoff. She had just left her husband Klaus Ranier Rohl, the publisher of the Czechoslovakian—subsidized magazine *Konkret*. They formed the Baader-Meinhoff gang. The year was 1968, the birthdate of terrorism as we know it. Baader was not on a vacation. He traveled to Bogota, Rome, and Zurich for the same purpose he went to Berlin for. This purpose was operational. It is reasonable to assume that Baader contacted other terrorist groups at this point. He met the ELN in Bogota, the Red Brigades in Italy and the Petra Krause group in Zurich.

"When Carlos killed the two French policemen and Michel Moukarbel in his Paris apartment, the police found he left behind an address book. One of the entries was *Carmela Sarmiento*. Who was Carmela Sarmiento? She was an 18 year old who was kidnapped in Bogota, Colombia, and held for over a year in an underground peoples' jail before she was released. On the day she was kidnapped, a French citizen, Bernard Courcelle, hastily caught a plane in Bogota and returned to Paris. Who was Bernard Courcelle? He was the boyfriend of the Sarmiento's maid. Who was the maid? The maid was a graduate of Lumumba University in Moscow where she first met Carlos. Who was Carlos? He was a Venezuelan terrorist in the pay of the Wadi Haddad of the Palestinian PFLP. Who was Wadi Haddad? He was part of the PLO which was funded by the Soviet Union.

"On his defection from the Revolutionary Cells, Hans-Joachim Klein confessed that the German guerrilla movements were no longer independent. Every decision, he said, had to be approved by Wadi

Haddad. And there was a price tag that the German terrorists paid. They had to participate in actions with the Palestinian terrorists. That is how, Klein said, the German terrorist became involved in operations such as Entebbe. The German terrorists needed money, and Klein revealed that the Revolutionary Cells received $3,000 every month plus cases of weapons. In return the Revolutionary Cells had—as Klein put it—a finger in the pie of the massacre at the Munich Olympics."

"The German 2 June Movement was also paid by the PFLP. One of its earliest contacts with the Palestinians was made when German terrorists belonging to all of the German groups, including the Baader-Meinhoff gang, trained in the large PFLP military training camp in Yemen. This camp is supported by Soviets, Cubans and East Germans who provide men, money and supplies.

"The Baader-Meinhoff gang worked with the PFLP in the seizure of the Air France flight that was diverted to Entebbe. They also participated in the hijacking of the Lufthansa flight to Mogadiscio.

"In the Netherlands, members of Dutch terrorist and quasi-terrorist groups were recruited for terrorist missions by the PFLP. One example was Luiwina Janssen, who was recruited to case the Lod airport in Tel Aviv in preparation for another massacre.

"In Ireland, France and Spain there are interconnecting links between the Provisional Irish Republican Army of Ireland, the Brittany Separatists of France and the ETA-V (of ETA-Militar) of Spain. These groups are tied to Cuba and can be identified as steadfast practitioners of the Foco theory of revolutionary warfare. All are trained in Cuba and in Libya where Cuban trainers are stationed. There is no way to appease these groups except complete capitulation. The ETA-V, for example, wants not Basque independence, but the eventual communication of Spain. There is little likelihood it will forsake this goal.

"Another Spanish terrorist group, GRAPO, was supplied with explosives by the Petra Krause group in Switzerland which also maintained a meeting site for the Red Brigades from Italy. Both the German 2 June Movement and the Revolutionary Cells maintained numerous safehouses in Northern Italy.

"The crimson web grows bigger and bigger and spreads to the United States. Black Panthers were trained in the same PLO training camps where the Baader-Meinhoff gang was trained—the same one which trained the IRA, the Revolutionary Cells, the Iranian Mujahidin and the Chariks. The Weatherman were trained in Cuba. On returning to the United States they published the Foco theory and the works of Carlos Marighella so that others might follow it. The present more potent FALN is also Cuba-trained and supported. There is no question about it. Cuba admits it.

"In the Near East the PLO has trained Iranian terrorists for the past ten years, beginning in 1970. The Iranian terrorist cadres were not only trained in terrorism and guerrilla warfare, but also participated alongside Palestinian units in armed forays into Israel. In 1978 the PLO secretly trained about 10,000 Iranian terrorists on orders from the Soviet Union. So great was their commitment to this training program that not one international terrorist incident of any sizeable dimension took place in that year. All members of the Palestinian groups, including the Rejectionist Front, participated. Even the PFLP-funded Japanese Red Army had its role. JRA members were sent to Cuba and the People's Democratic Republic of Yemen to assist in the training programs. In view of this triangle of support involving the Soviet Union, the PLO (a communist organization) and communist Iranian terrorists, it seems quite unlikely that multinational corporations will be allowed to continue doing business in Iran, or even hold on to their investments.

"The main coordinating point for worldwide terrorism today strongly appears to be in the People's Democratic Republic of Yemen (PDRY). The Soviets are stockpiling weapons in the PDRY, long ago surpassing the needs of the 10,000 man PDRY army. Also available in the PDRY are Cuban, Soviet, East German and PLO advisors, plus the moral support and guidance of the Communist Bloc. For one week each month, the PDRY is visited by delegations of highly-ranked Soviet officials. At the moment this terrorist coalition is primarily concerned with training the Popular Front for the Liberation of Oman (PFLO).

"In Latin America every major terrorist organization has been trained in Cuba and today continues to receive advice, guidance, and support from Cuba. In the Caribbean, Cuba has already supervised the overthrow of Grenada, reportedly by sending a 10 man guerrilla squad to help the local insurgents capture the police station, and is reaching for Jamaica. Presently the security services of Jamaica are being trained by the Cuban service, indicative that Jamaica will soon be absorbed.

"The crimson web extends from one point to another and then comes back again to fortify itself. For instance, one of the first international revolutionaries to surface in Managua after the fall of Nicaragua was Regis Debray—in whose apartment Andreas Baader stayed in 1968 the year this began.

"This most important consideration in assessing current overseas risk to the United States, its people and its businesses is burgeoning worldwide insurgency. This risk is not based upon economic or social problems, but on a foreign power's desire for military conquest . . . through a crimson web of terror."

Appendix

CLASSIFICATION OF TERRORIST ORGANIZATIONS

Traditional Homeland Liberation Organizations with Single Targets

1. Croatian Separatists. **Target:** Yugoslavian Government Officials.
2. Armenian Liberation Army. **Target:** Turkish Government Officials.
3. South Moluccans. **Targets:** Dutch and Indonesian Officials. Hostage Taking.
4. Movement for the Self-Determination and Independence of The Canary Archipelago. **Target:** Spanish Government.
5. Basque Homeland and Freedom. **Target:** Spanish Government (FOCO Theory).
6. Irish Republican Army. **Targets:** Irish Protestants and British (FOCO Theory).
7. Britanny Separatist Front. **Target:** French Government (FOCO).

International Third Country Organizations with Multi-Targets*

1. Popular Front for The Liberation of Palestine.

*International groups use multiple targetting against all nationalities except the USSR Bloc. All use the same tactics, such as hostage taking.

2. Black September.
3. Popular Front for the Liberation of Palestine - General Command.
4. Front for the Liberation of Palestine.
5. Black June.
6. Arab Liberation Front.
7. Japanese Red Army.

Anti-Establishment Internal Organizations with Multi-Targets

1. Baader-Meinhoff Targets: German, United States (FOCO Theory).
2. 2 June Movement Multi-Targets: German, United States (FOCO Theory).
3. Revolutionary Cells Multi-Targets (FOCO Theory).
4. Red Resistance Front Multi-Targets: Dutch, German, United States (FOCO Theory).
5. 17 November Group Multi-Targets: Greek, United States (FOCO Theory).
6. Red Brigades Multi-Targets: Italian and United States (FOCO Theory).

Guerrilla/Terrorist Movements

1. Turkish People's Liberation Party/Front-Swift Ones Multi-Targets: Turks, United States.
2. New People's Army Targets: Philippine Government, United States.
3. Moro National Liberation Front Multi-Targets: Philippine, all other nationalities.
4. All African National Liberation Movements.
5. Guerrilla Army of the Poor Multi-Targets (FOCO Theory).
6. Revolutionary Armed Forces Multi-Targets (FOCO Theory).
7. Colombian Revolutionary Armed Force Multi-Targets.

8. Popular Liberation Army Multi-Targets.
9. Sandinist National Liberation Front Multi-Targets (FOCO Theory).
10. Joint Revolutionary Command Multi Targets (FOCO Theory).
11. 23 September Communist League Multi-Targets (FOCO Theory).
12. Tupamaros Multi-Targets (FOCO Theory).
13. People's Revolutionary Army Multi-Targets (FOCO Theory).
14. People's Struggler Multi-Targets: Iranian Officials, United States (FOCO Theory).
15. People's Sacrifice Guerrilla's Single Target: Iranian.